New Perspectives
Coastal Houses

Author: Arian Mostaedi
Publisher: Carles Broto
Editorial Coordinator: Cristina Soler
Architectural Adviser: Eduard Malgosa
Graphic Design: Oriol Vallès Garcia
Text: contributed by the architects

Edition 2007

© Carles Broto i Comerma
Jonqueres, 10, 1-5
08003 Barcelona, Spain
Tel.: +34 93 301 21 99
 Fax: +34-93-301 00 21
E-mail: info@linksbooks.net
www. linksbooks.net

All rights reserved. No part of this book may be used or reproduced in any manner whatsoever without written permission except in the case of brief quotations embodied in critical articles and reviews.

New Perspectives
Coastal Houses

Index

8 **Anne Lacaton & Jean Philippe Vassal.** *House in Lege*

16 **Anne Marie Sumner.** *Own House*

28 **Brian Healy.** *Beach House*

40 **Carlos Herrera.** *House in Acapulco / House in Huatulco*

56 **Fernau & Hartman Architects, Inc.** *Anderson / Ayers House*

66 **Gray Organschi.** *Tennis House*

76 **Helliwell + Smith Blue Sky Architecture.** *Greenwood House*

84 **Henri Edouard Ciriani.** *Playa Escondida House*

96 **Jackson Clements Burrows Pty Ltd Architects.** *Riverside Terrace*

104 **Jarmund / Vigsnæs AS Architects MNAL.** *Summer Cabin on the Coast of Norway*

120 **Jordi Garcés.** *House in Costa Brava*

132 **José Cruz Ovalle.** *House in Santo Domingo*

142 **Josep Lluís Mateo & Arturo Vila.** House in Artà

154 **Legorreta + Legorreta.** House La Cruz

160 **MVRDV.** Borneo Houses

174 **Niall McLaughlin.** Northamptonshire Shack

182 **Pete Bossley.** House in Bay of Islands

188 **Philip Gumuchdjian.** D.P. Think Tank / Boathouse

198 **Richard Francis-Jones.** Two houses in Woy Woy

210 **Sandra Barclay & Jean-Pierre Crousse.** House B

220 **Silvia Gmür & Livio Vacchini.** 3 Single—Family

230 **Stan Bolt.** O'Sullivan House

240 **TEN Arquitectos.** House IA

250 **Toshiko Mori.** Cohen House

Introduction

Water has always been a major attraction and a popular site for locating residences. Seas and rivers have been great sources of wealth and resources, and have led to the emergence and development of many towns and cities all over the world.

At the present time, the aquatic world is also an ideal framework in which to spend one's holidays or to lead a peaceful life in a landscape that maintains a close dialogue with the individual. Water is at the same time soothing and uncontrollable, involving immensity and variation. It acts as a mirror that multiplies the landscape, it illuminates spaces with its reflections and it contributes a countless range of shades that provide its admirers with a great variety of sensations.

This book presents some of the schemes located on the coasts and riverbanks of the earth, They show the efforts of their designers to conceive an architecture that is elegant, appropriate to its environment and able to provide its inhabitants with the necessary comfort and security to enjoy a stimulating interaction with nature. These unusual works are located on seas, oceans, rivers and lakes but do not damage their idyllic image of natural paradises. Fortunately, respect for the environment and care to avoid aggressive visual impacts are increasingly influential factors in the design of buildings that are intended as something more than a simple inhabitable space. These buildings are dream houses for many people, the refuge to which they can retreat from the stress of modern life. The architects organise the spaces to take full advantage of their location and to create a dialogue with the interior and the exterior of the building so that the two concepts are often merged into one. The aspects that are given most emphasis by the architects that appear in this selection are the use of appropriate and sturdy materials that can withstand the latent violence of water, the arrangement of elements or structures that provide refreshing shade for hot summer days, the incorporation of pools as elements that benefit both the inhabitants and the dwellings, and the careful selection of colours and textures for the facades. Each architect deals with these elements in their own way, showing their distinctive touch and representing the demands of the clients and the site. This is an architecture created for a blue world in which the seas, rivers and lakes determine their final configuration and in which the distant harmonious horizon seems to be closer than ever.

Anne Lacaton & Jean Philippe Vassal
House in Lege
Cap Ferret, France

Photographs: Philippe Ruault

This dwelling is in a wonderful location, giving directly onto Arcachon Bay and the Atlantic Ocean to the west of Bordeaux. It is a privileged space, one of the last undeveloped plots in an area with magnificent views over the water. Due to the characteristics of the land, an extension of sand dunes whose crest is 15 m above the level of the water, populated by fifty pines rising to 30 m, the architects made an effort to design a building that was able to adapt to and take advantage of its environment. The client brief consisted in building a dwelling on this site without damaging the environment and its qualities. The project maintains the density of the forest —no trees were cut down— and respects the natural undulation of the ground. Six trees go through the house. On the roof, transparent plane plastic sheets are tightened to the trunks with flexible rubber. They can glide on the edges of holes in the roof when the trees are moving with the wind.

The house is a platform of 210 sqm on a single level, built on pillars 2 to 4 metres high according to the slope of the land. This makes it possible to pass under the house and to have better views of the landscape from the interior of the dwelling. The structure is made of steel and the facades are of corrugated aluminium with openings of corrugated transparent fibreglass panels. The lower surface of the floor slab is covered with the same corrugated aluminium, which reflects the light reflected on the water. Finally, the front facade facing Arcachon Bay was left totally transparent, with sliding glass doors.

Longitudinal section

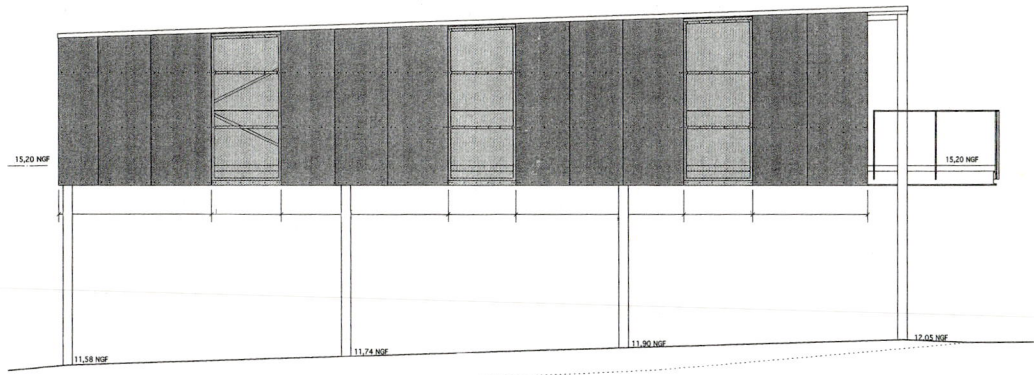

West elevation

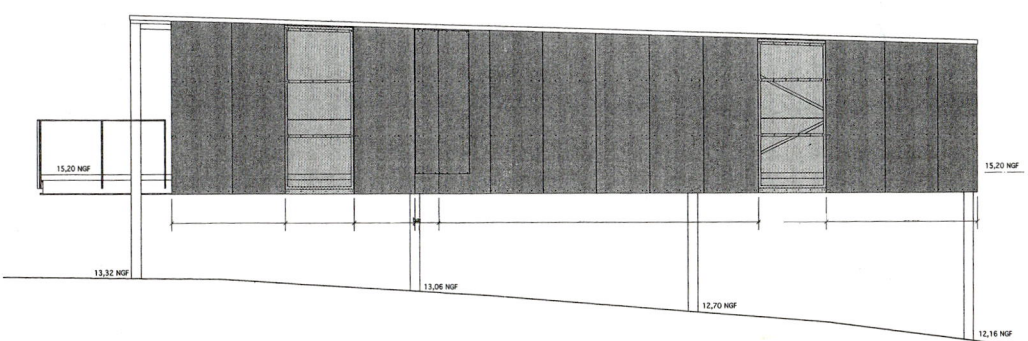

East elevation

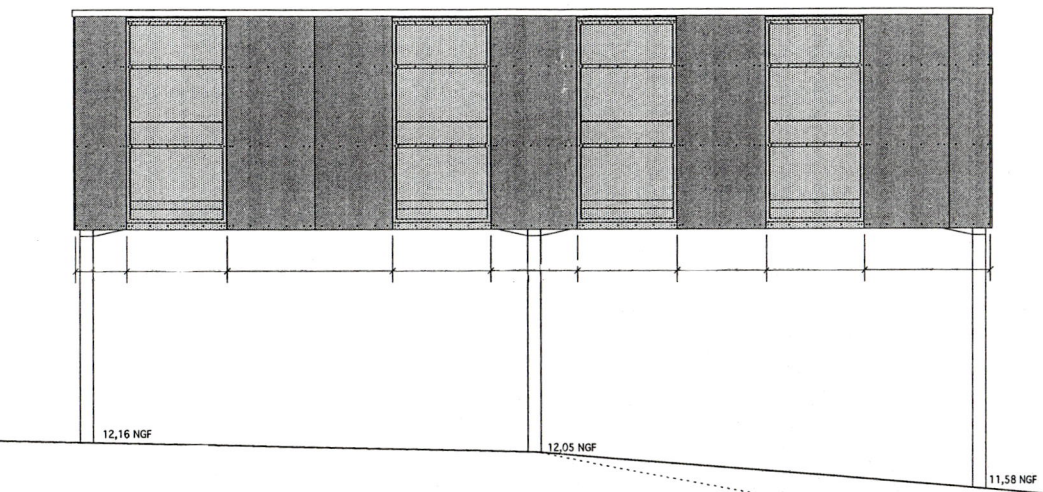

North elevation

Own House

Sao Paulo, Brazil

Photographs: Nelson Kon

The architect Marie Sumner chose the coast of Sao Paulo to realise the dream of all architects: their own house, specially designed and located in a very special place. This dwelling located on the edge of the sea with spectacular views shows a love for nature, and especially for the marine landscape. In addition to being the home of Marie Sumner, it is a design that helps one to understand the intentions of her architecture, which reflects the concerns of Brazilian architects in recent decades.

Taking advantage of the sloping land on which it is located, the house is structured as a horizontal plane that stands out minimally, fitting like an oasis in the middle of the forest with its blue colour, halfway between the lightness of the sky and the serenity of the sea. With the creation of wide openings in its facades it was possible to accentuate the tension between transparencies and opacities, and several spatial complicities arose between the interior and the exterior of the building.

This house also presents interesting informal features in the distribution of the atmospheres, and in the stratagems used to communicate the different levels. For example, the circulation of the bedrooms located on the lower floor is independent, external and always open to the landscape. To integrate the two sides of the dwelling, a large corridor was excavated to communicate with the living room located on the upper level, which is accessed by means a staircase that emerges from the floor just beside the chimney. A whole series of details help to simplify and give functionality to a project in which the architecture uses the land and the landscape as a framework for its expressive richness. The culmination of this expressiveness is appreciated in the almost invisible layout of the elements on the upper floor, where the large living room merges with the solarium located on the roof of the bedrooms. A second staircase provides direct access from the solarium to the south wing of the bedrooms, while the north wing connects to the track that goes down to the beach through the forest. The solarium, which has shade provided by an isolated porch, is like a piazza suspended in the air that forms a magnificent window onto a landscape in which the forest meets the sea.

In this project it was not intended to use mimetic effects or local building elements, but to emphasise the contrast between the building and its environment.

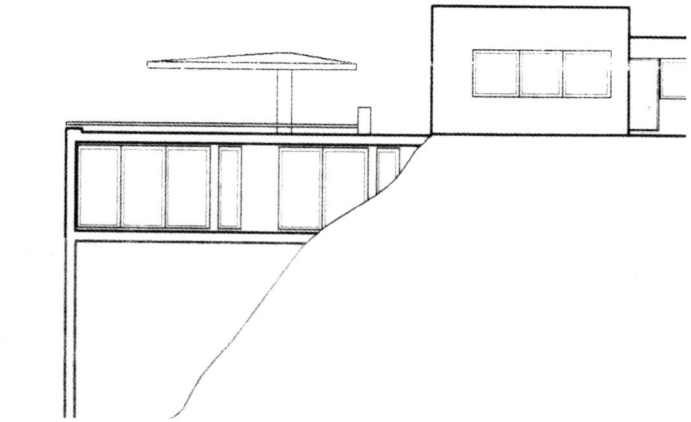

Northeast elevation

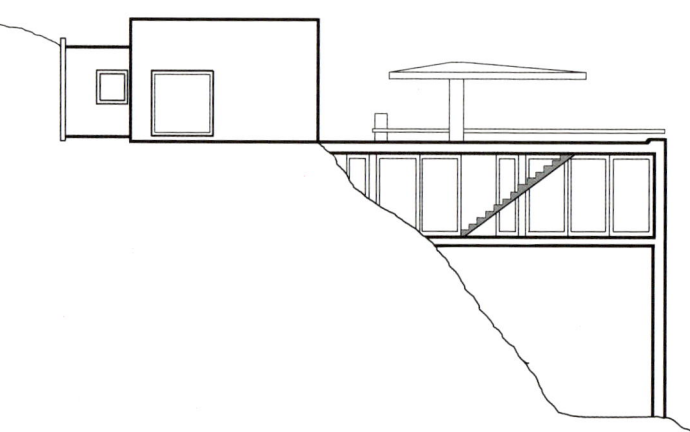

Southeast elevation

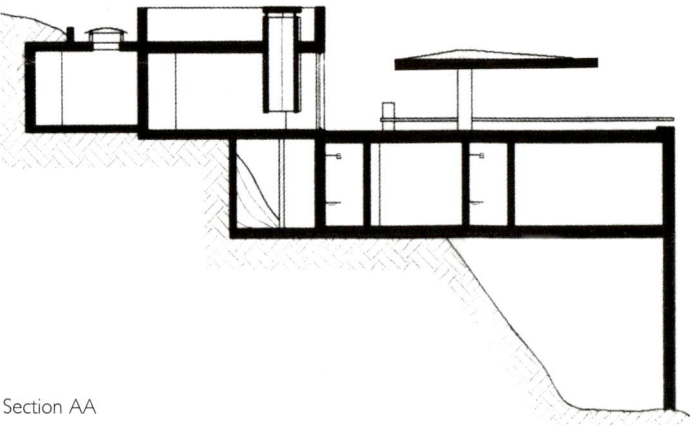

Section AA

The simple forms and the formal synthesis are emphasised by the large spaces in this dwelling. The change of colour between the exterior and the interior contrasts with the continuity of the mosaic floor with details in basalt. In some places the granite rock on which the house was built has been left exposed.

Beach House

Loveladies, New Jersey, USA

Photographs: Paul Warchol

This house is located on Long Beach Island, which acts as a natural barrier for the nearby central coast of New Jersey and is generally used for holidays. The site on which it was built is in the north of the island, at the end of a country road that goes over the dunes leading to the beach.

In siting the building the architects sought to relate the structure of the dwelling with its environment. By means of overlapping volumes, geometries, materials and colours, the building acts as a mediator between the street wall and the horizontal ocean, with a daring and stimulating aesthetics full of intelligent details that contribute new readings of the role of contemporary architecture.

At one end the house is oriented towards the ocean, so in order to maximise the effect of the landscape, it was decided to open it completely. The marine facade is made entirely of glass, although it has a lattice of wooden slats that acts as a sun filter. Here the main living area was raised one level in order to take better advantage of the views and sea breezes. At the other end, the facade meets the street and its openings are more discreet. However, contrary to conventional practice there is a space for walkers who come down to the beach: a public bench located at the entrance to the beach that allows the street to participate in the building, thus questioning the prejudices of privacy.

In the interior layout, the different spaces are articulated according to the composition of the different volumes of the dwelling. A glazing pavilion of double height contains the social spaces and the main bedroom on the upper level whose interior window communicates with the living room. The guest rooms and the secondary bedrooms are housed in a second wing or "motel" that occupies the two floors on the west side of the building.

This house is located right on the beach, so it has splendid views of the Atlantic Ocean.

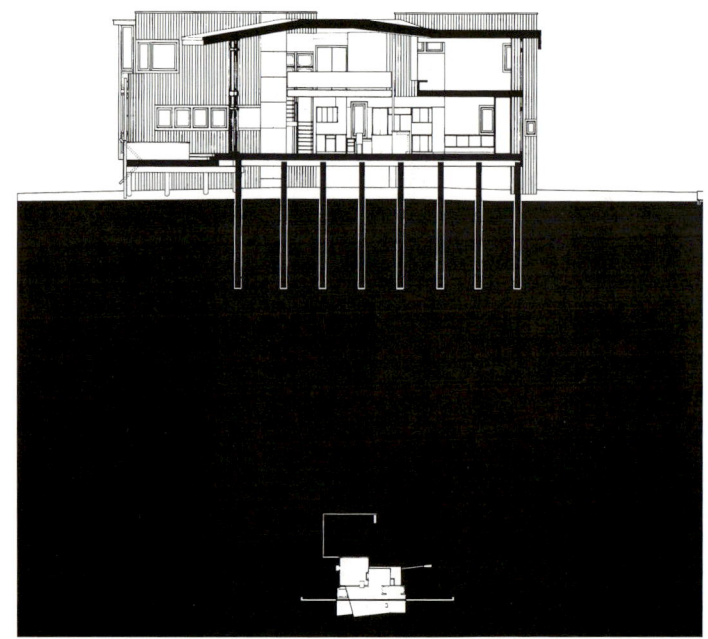

Cross section

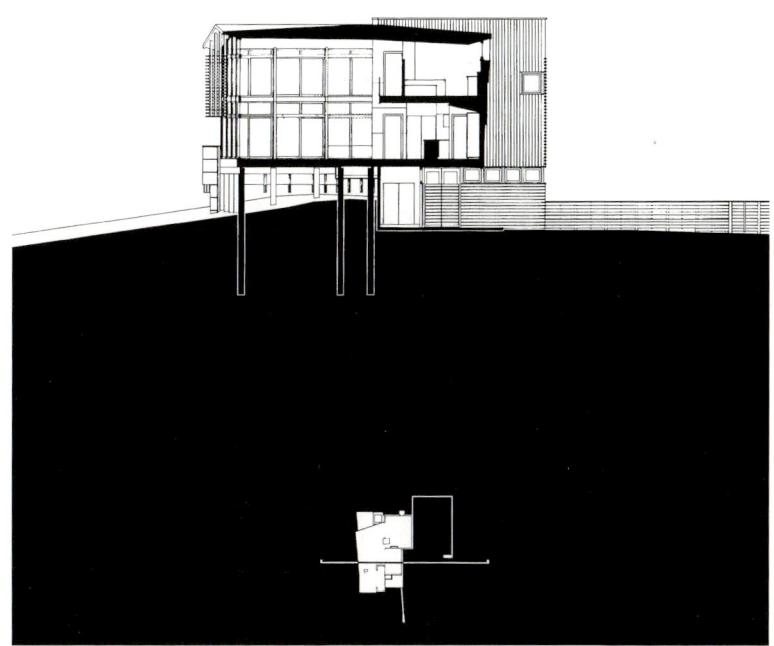

Longitudinal section

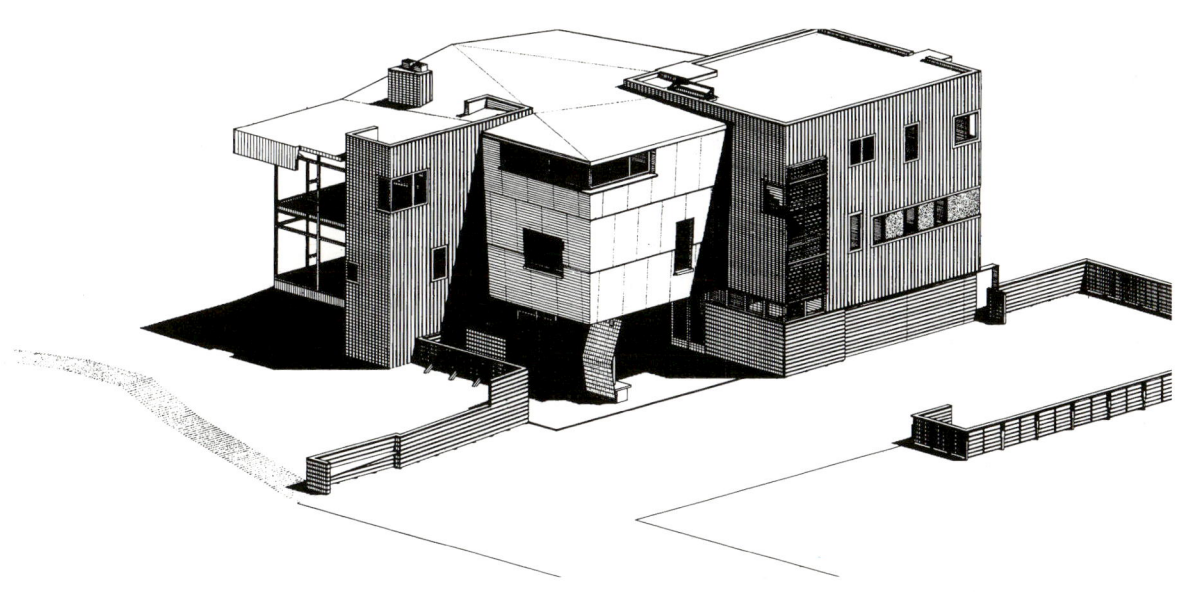

House in Acapulco / House in Huatulco
Acapulco / Oaxaca, Mexico

Photographs: Shanon Fernández, Lilia Schnaas / Jaime Jacott

The architect Carlos Herrera designed two interesting schemes on the Mexican coast, The first one, a residence located in Las Brisas (Acapulco), serves as an example of contemporary Mexican architecture. Its rich formal simplicity is based on large spaces that dictate and maintain the proportion and symmetry. The sensation of harmony and balance are achieved thanks to the careful arrangement of the governing element of this composition. A canvas awning with the pure white line of its catenary and its monumental support creates a forceful and spectacular space that seems to float on the wonderful blue horizon of the sea and forms the point of convergence and interrelation of all the atmospheres of the dwelling. The architectural solution offers a balanced mixture of the conservative and the modern. The living room and dining room are open, formal spaces full of comfort, whereas the sober pool area is simpler and more informal.

In the second scheme, the dwelling is set on a hill at the south-east end of Tangolunda Bay (Oaxaca), an authentic paradise due to its excellent climate. The plot is in an incomparable location, though it has a steep slope and a narrow front. The house adopts the longitudinal orientation of the site in a well-linked succession of spaces that are tied in a profound geometric rigor that is expressed through triangles.

The design includes several expressions from the current architectural language that seeks formal simplicity and minimises the elements, but creates its own particular aesthetic code. It is an architecture that is described as one walks through it, giving the itinerary an active value that allows its strict postulates to be discovered through the pleasant solutions. Its configuration and its close relationship with the environment is dictated by a clear compositional axis that creates a sequence preceded by a covered parking space leading to an access courtyard. This familiar element in Mexican architecture here takes a new form framed by three walls that rise next to the palms and are crowned by a celestial vault. The access gradually opens the perspective toward the social area of the house, which forms a powerful frame for the beauty of the Pacific Ocean.

The dwelling has an appropriate orientation that provides a great degree of thermal comfort controlled with passive environmental conditioning.

The house is developed in successive descending levels. From the social area one descends to the bedrooms through an open courtyard that allows the bedrooms to flow and mix with the colours of the garden.

On the lower terrace, a velarium covers the visitors without blocking the wind and brings the architecture closer to nature.

The decoration is in tune with the architectural design and maintains a perfect scale with the internal courtyards and large volumes.

From the entrance one can see the carefully shaped stone elements that are placed according to a rhythmic sequence of gardens and architectural figures, seeming to delineate the land of which they form part.

The interior spaces are of an austere domestic architecture with simple and cool materials and good, open construction solutions that form atmospheres that intermingle with the natural environment and complement it.

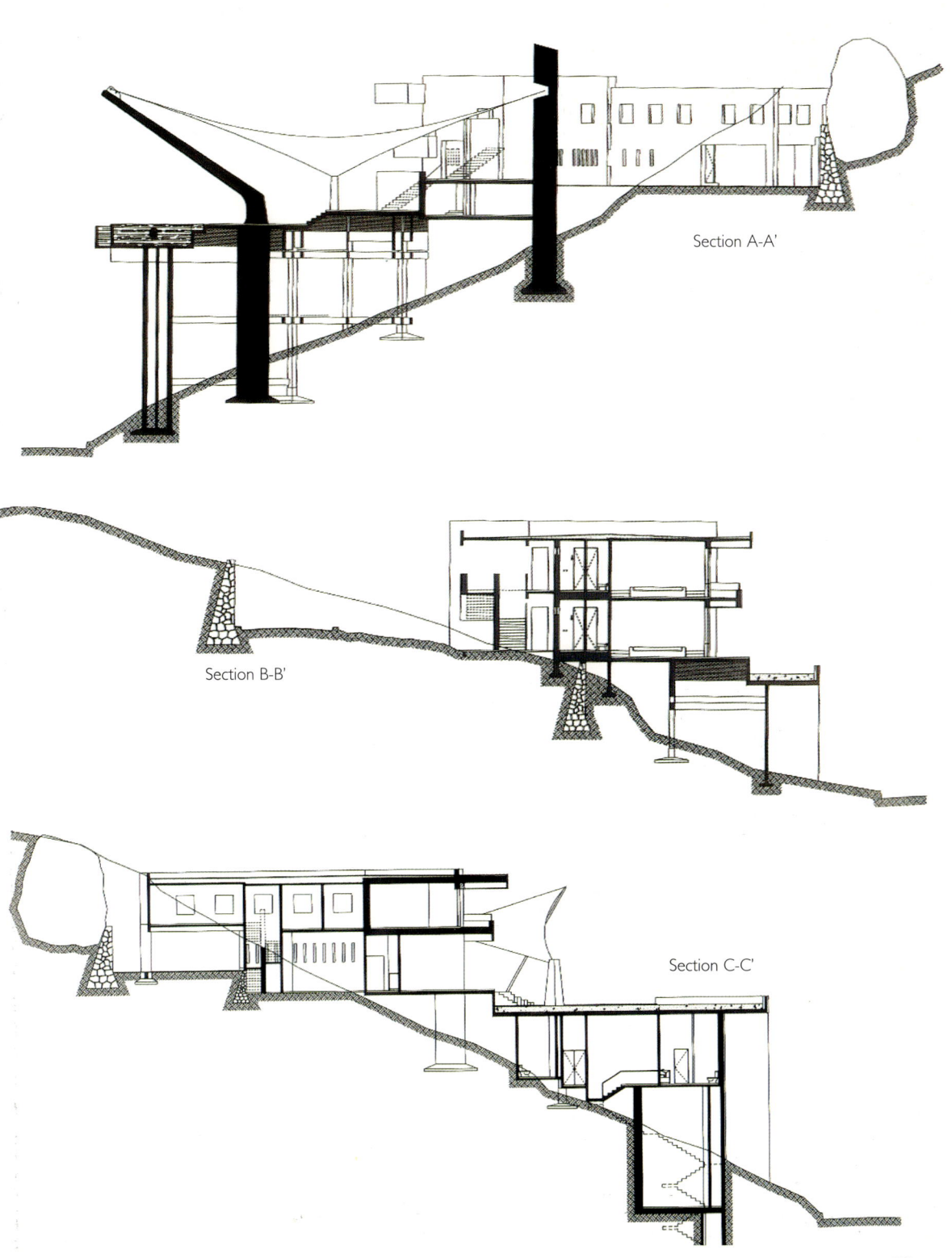

On the lower terrace, a velarium covers the visitors without blocking the wind and brings the architecture closer to nature.

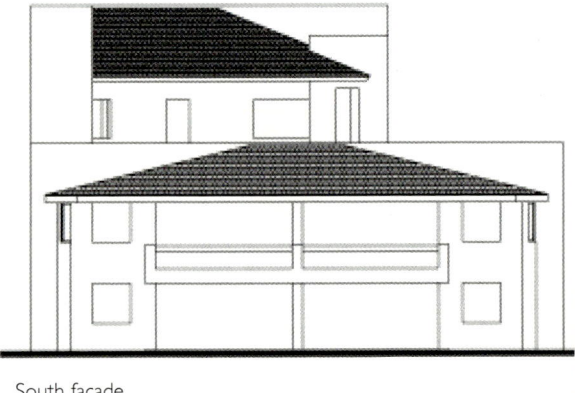

South facade

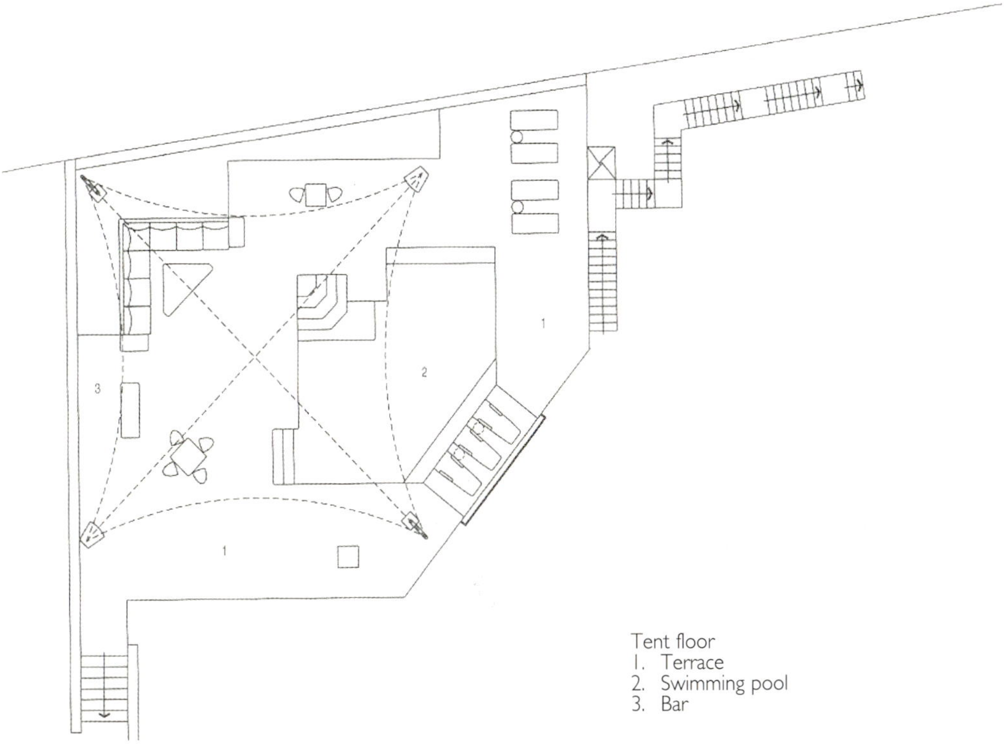

Tent floor
1. Terrace
2. Swimming pool
3. Bar

Fernau & Hartman Architects, Inc.
Anderson / Ayers House
Nicasio, California, USA

Photographs: Richard Barnes

The architectural language common to the area —agricultural buildings with vaulted barns and improvised henhouses— was the basis used to design the Anderson Ayers House. This dwelling is located on a sloping plot surrounded by hills, with views of a reservoir surrounded by fields and of the Pacific Ocean in the background. Although it is often a very sunny place, the local microclimate is subject to harsh winds and fog that can be very uncomfortable during the rainy months of autumn and winter.

The scheme was articulated around the formal and informal compositional strategies, the formal ones referring to the idealised world and the informal ones referring to the world as it is and as it appears. The common language, the expression of the architecture of the street, was the main source of inspiration for the informal adaptive strategies. However, bearing in mind that the circumstantial architecture alternately accepts and manipulates the conditions that define an architectural situation, the formal intentions were rewritten in order to adapt them to the immediate circumstances. Their design could therefore begin with a formal strategy that was later "remodelled" conceptually to adapt it to the impositions of the location and of the client.

The dwelling is the second residence of a couple of artists with children whose desire was to live in a "barn-theatre" — outwardly introverted and inwardly open. As the place is exposed and is potentially visible from the distance, it was decided, after several analyses, to divide the house into two wings: one housing the study, the pool and dressing rooms, and one housing the main spaces of the dwelling. The main living room is a barrel vaulted "bar" that is situated. across the slope and oriented so that the roof shelters it from the wind. This wing is lightly stepped, thus naturally creating the inclination of a theatre, with a common stage-like space in the centre and the kitchen and the main bedroom occupying the spaces to the left and right. The room with the vaulted roof is for this dwelling the structure, or the "chart" as they say in Jazz, around which the other elements are improvised. The secondary rooms are then like "riffs" that modify and reinterpret the whole. The final result is a work in which one appreciates the genuine character of the environment, the effects of an incidental aesthetics and the magic of an improvising method.

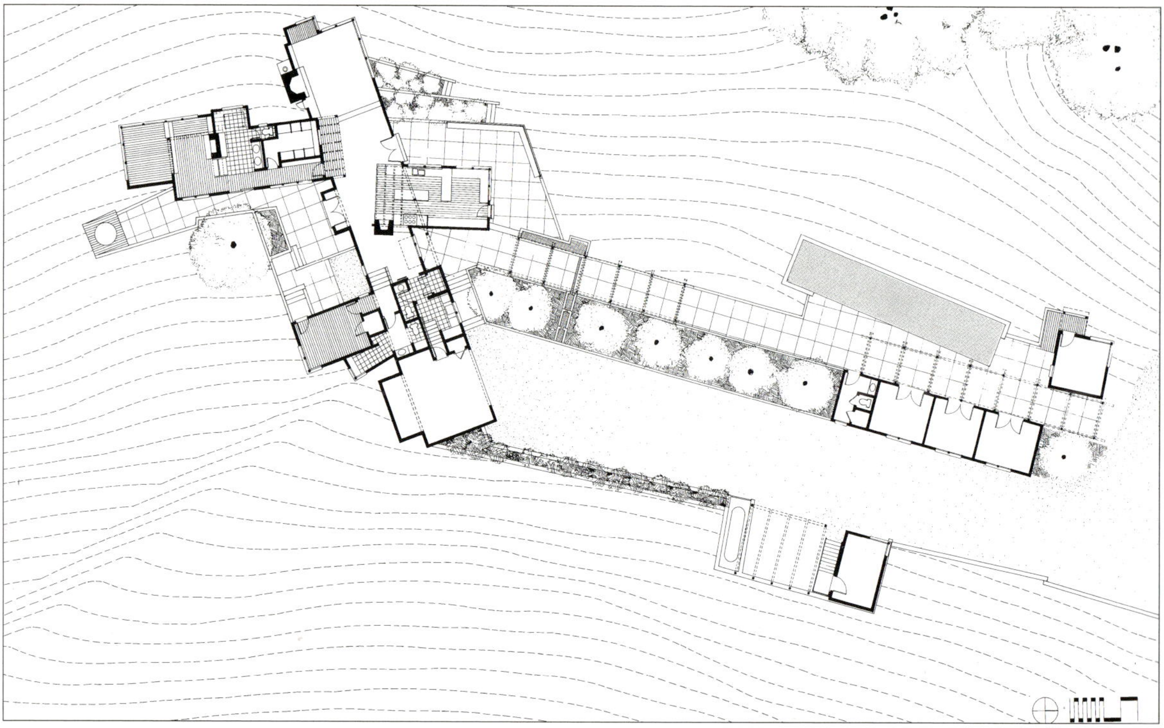

58

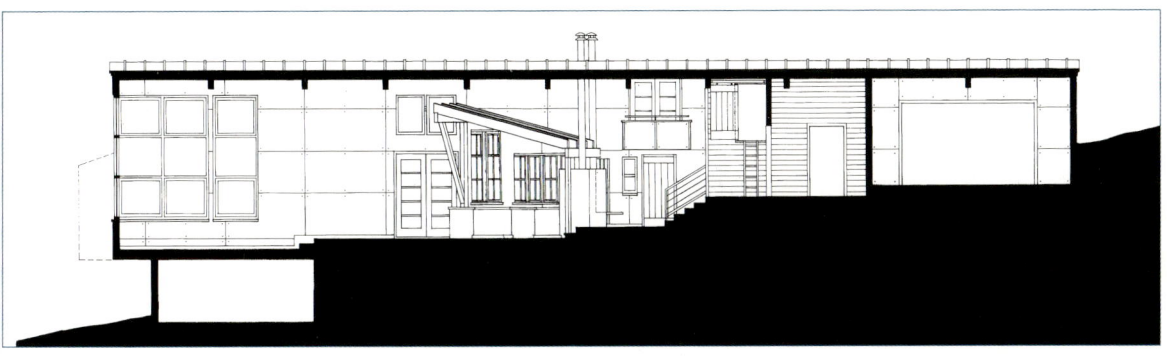

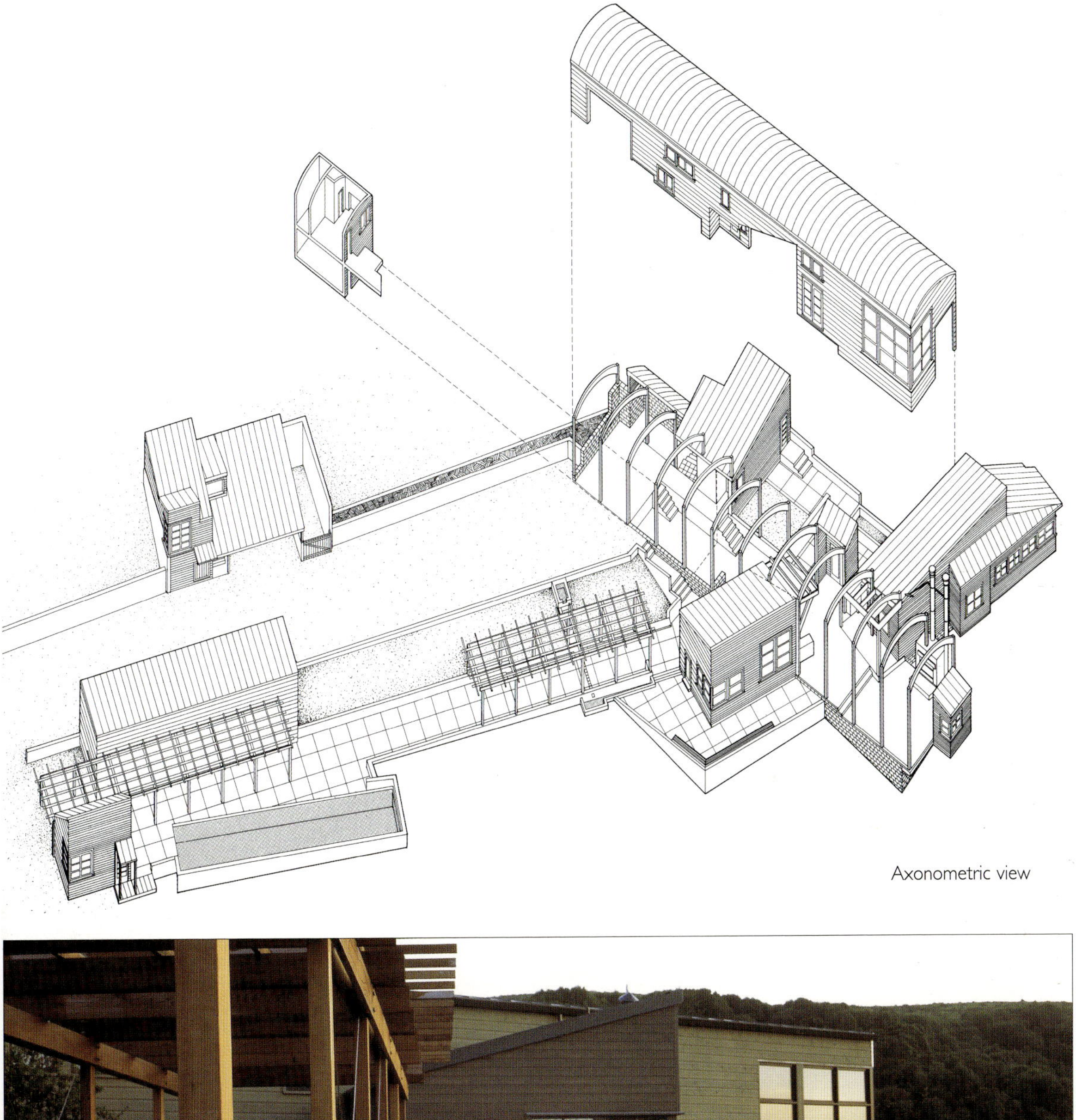

Axonometric view

In the space of the living room, the curved form of the ceiling leaves a small hole through which the light illuminates the interior spaces.

The large windows also contributes to the natural lighting, offering the visual spectacle of excellent views.

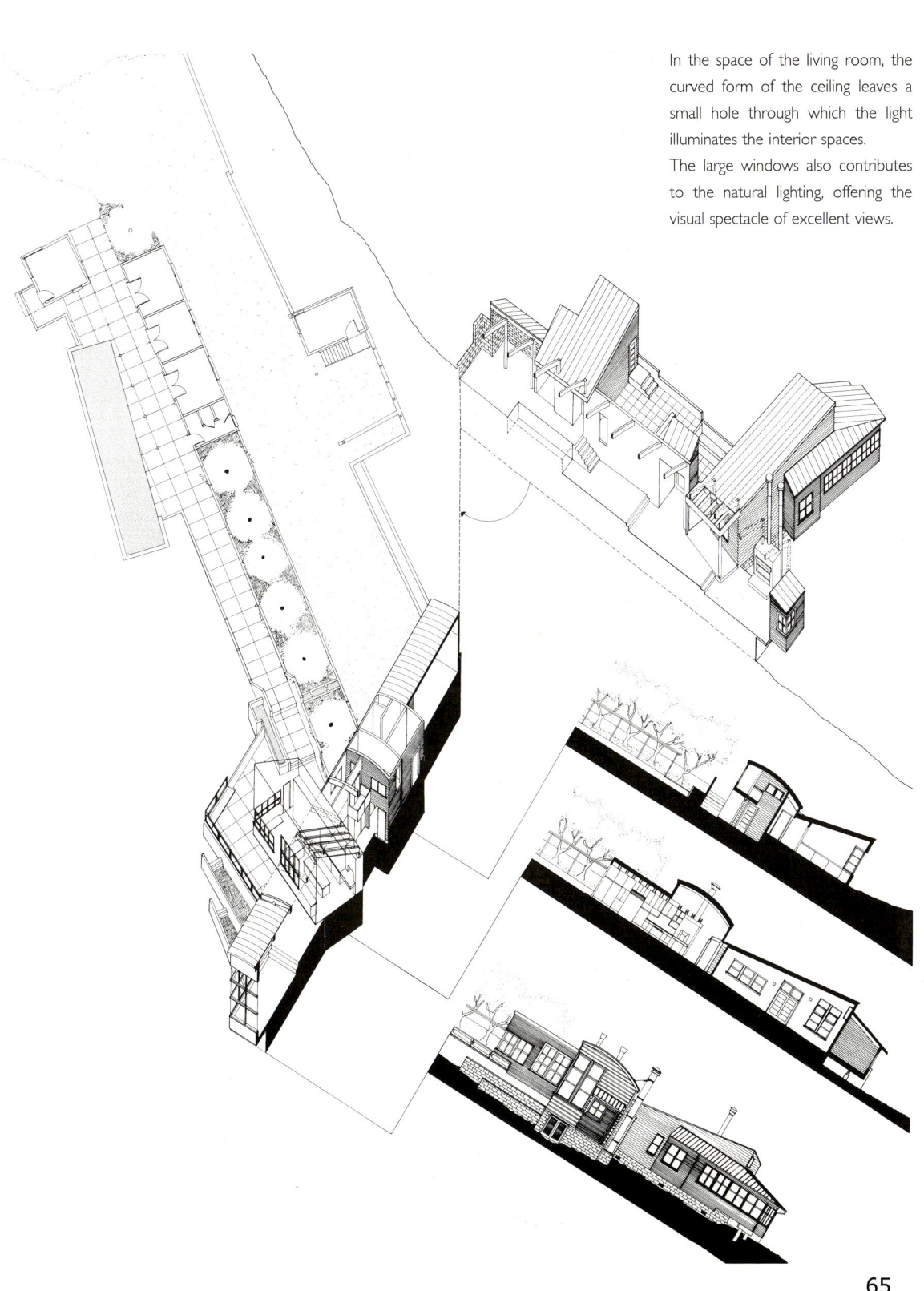

Gray Organschi
Tennis House
Connecticut, USA

Photographs: Edward Hueber

Tennis House forms part of a large forest area in the north-west of the state of Connecticut. The building is located at the end of a small valley, on a site that was formerly a gravel pit but now, after the discovery of an underground spring, is occupied by a pond surrounded by wild grasslands.

In the design of this property the architects aimed to negotiate the relationship between the qualities of the site and the creation of a garden, in which a tennis court is the main feature.

Because the lands at the end of the valley were protected by recent environmental regulations, the habitable spaces of the building had to comply with the legal limits. However, the clients presented an ambitious scheme that included two dressing rooms, a bathroom, service rooms, a kitchen with utility room, a pantry, a bedroom with bunks and a living room at the level of the tennis court. The court has retaining walls made of concrete blocks on three of its sides, leaving open the side furthest from the dwelling with views of the pond. Clover and vetch were planted up to the edges of these walls, giving lightness to elements that tend to offer a very solid appearance. The tennis court looks as if it had been cut cleanly out of the land, and is aligned at the same level as the surface of the pond. Overlooking the court at its south end, the dwelling is embedded into the hillside. The concrete retaining wall that forms the building's back elevation transforms along its lenght to create an exterior shower, a sink counter for the bathroom, a storage wallcontaining the kitchenette and laundry, a rear staircase, an interior fireplace and exterior grill, and ultimately a catch basin fot the roof's rainwater runoff.

Along the facade facing the tennis court, ten columns and a "box" of cypress wood that contains the dressing rooms and the indoor shower support the roof, which is trapezoidal and has a low corner from which the rainwater can drain off. This roof was covered with vegetation, forming a pure plane of grass that is only interrupted by the chimney and a skylight that illuminates the dressing rooms. The architects sought to reduce the thickness and weight of a roof of this type by placing between the membrane of fireproof insulation and the earth layer a plastic net that retains the water and allows it to drain off during heavy rainfall. This constant reserve means that it is practically unnecessary to water the grass and that the amount of earth used was considerably reduced. With that same ecological mentality, the building is heated and cooled by a geothermal pump that uses the thermal waters of the pond as a source of energy.

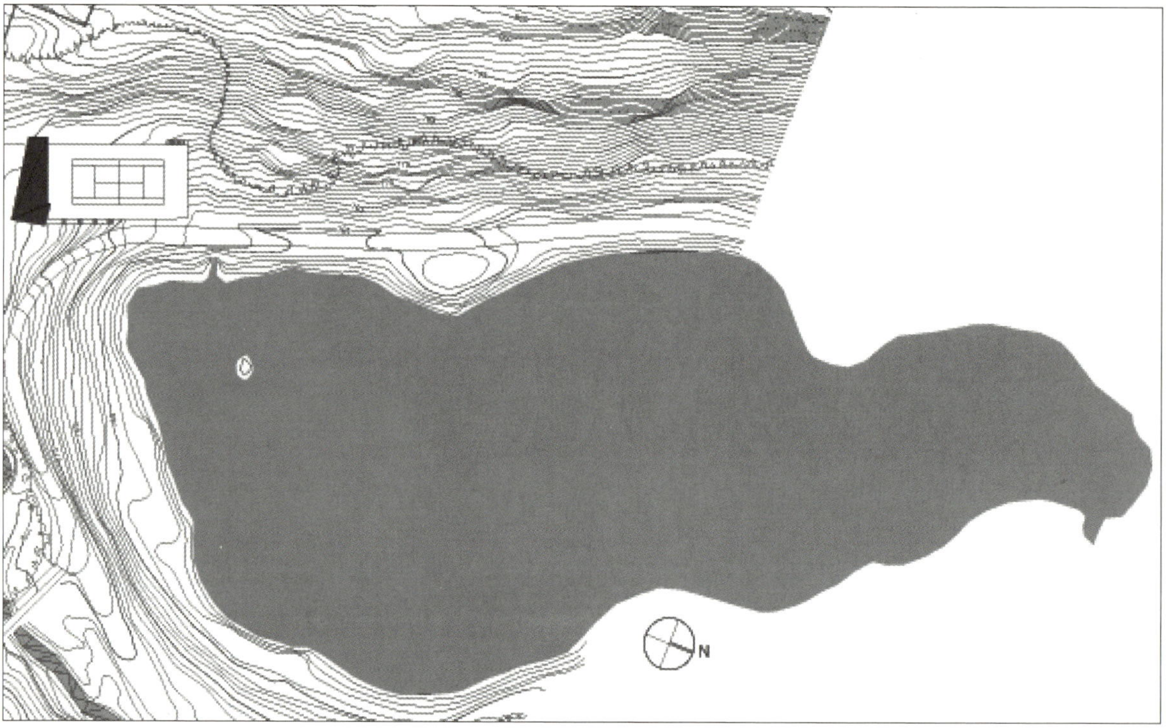

Site plan

The two walls that define the tennis court lengthways adapt to the natural elevations of the site, with steps going down the hill.

The dwelling is articulated around the tennis court and the pond, so from the main living areas, such as the living room and the terrace on the upper floor, one can enjoy the views or watch a tennis match.

Axonometric view

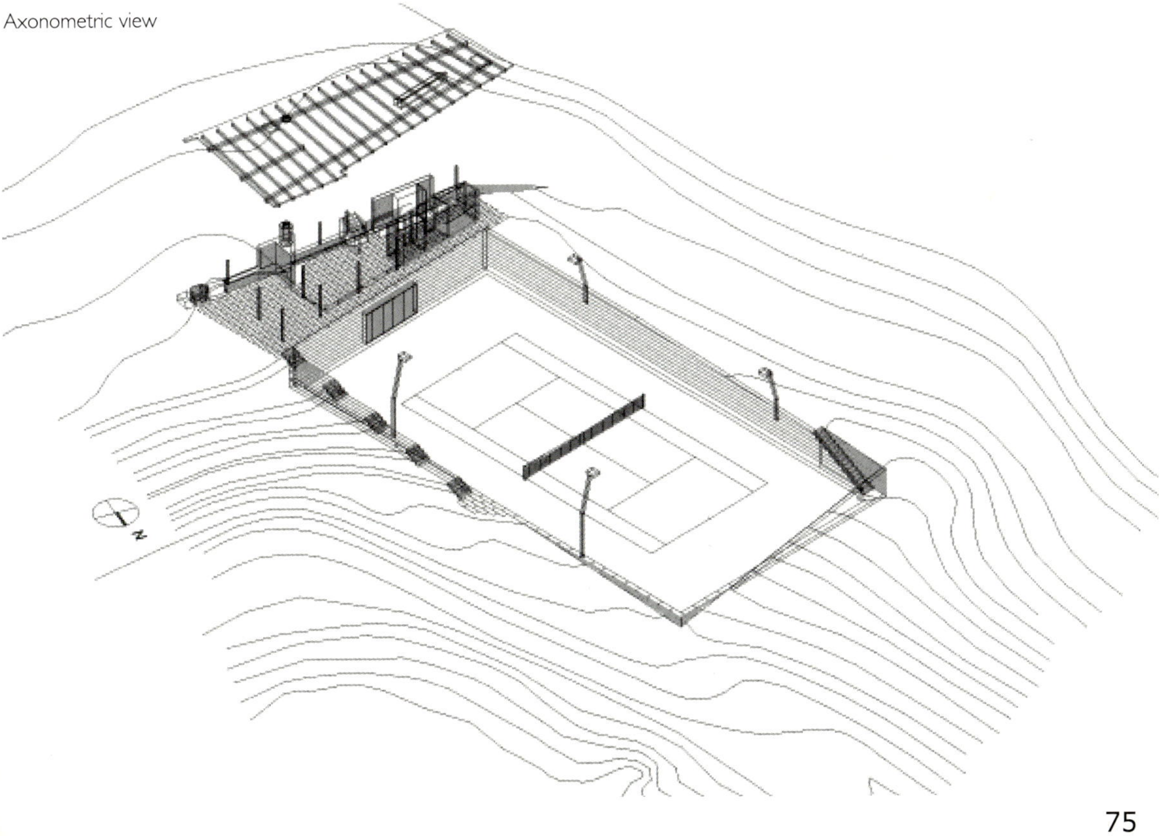

Helliwell + Smith Blue Sky Architecture
Greenwood House
Galiano Island, Canada

Photographs: Peter Powles, John Fulker

This dwelling is located on a strip of flat land on the northwest side of the island of Galiano, one of the Canadian islands in the Gulf of British Columbia. It has an excellent situation, between the waters of the Trincomali Channel to the southwest and the dense forest to the north-east. The building was to be sited far from the adjacent highway and from the effects of the high tide, so it was decided that it would have a linear composition, following the profile of the coast. Parallel to the coastline, a single row of beams of 40 cm diameter act as the dorsal fin of a structural skeleton. This frame, modulated continuously by pairs of crosspieces of 25 cm diameter, appears as a rhythmic succession of trunks that give form to the whole, with the roof standing out slightly at each end, providing a set of covered exterior spaces. The movements of the roof on the side facing the sea are calibrated with the sea views to take full advantage of the reflections of light and the vegetation, and to provide shade on the forest side. This structural system extends toward the landscape with a form that recalls the silhouette of a long dorsal fin. The rhythm of the structure of the roof connects to the floor by means of an orderly series of interior columns that run through the whole length of the building. The partitions between the columns organise the layout to generate the smaller spaces. To reinforce the divisions of the dwelling even further, the floors were given different surface treatments. In the bedrooms and living rooms they are paved with cherry colour floorboards, while the entrance to the kitchen and the service areas are united by a strip of stone tiles.

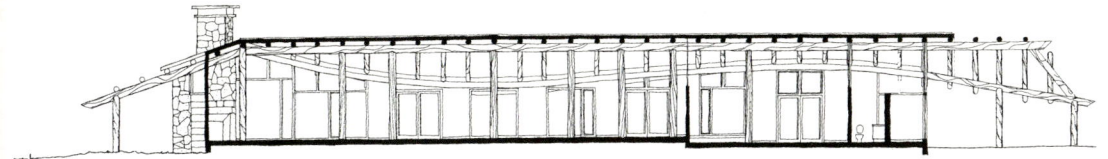

Longitudinal section looking towards the sea

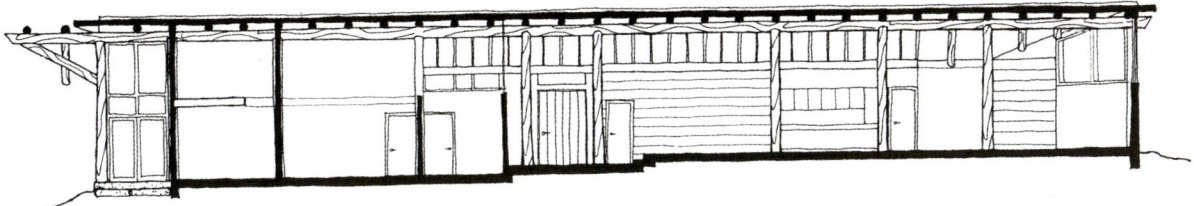

Longitudinal section along structural spine

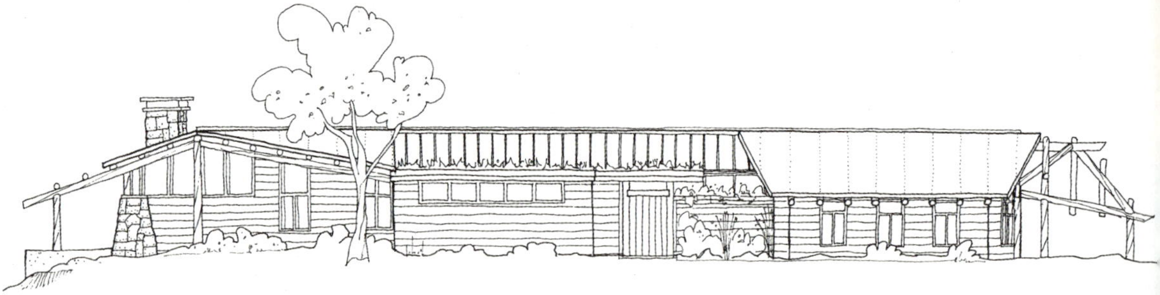

North-east elevation

South-east elevation

North-west elevation

To increase the interior lighting and to provide coolness, a continuous skylight provides speckled light filtered through the nearby trees.

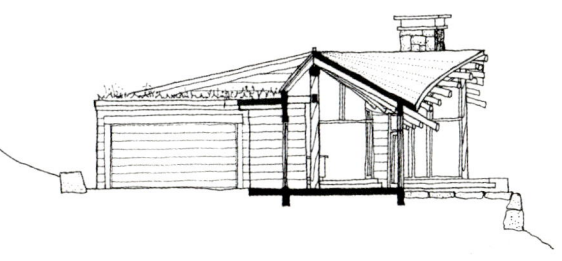

Longitudinal section through entrance

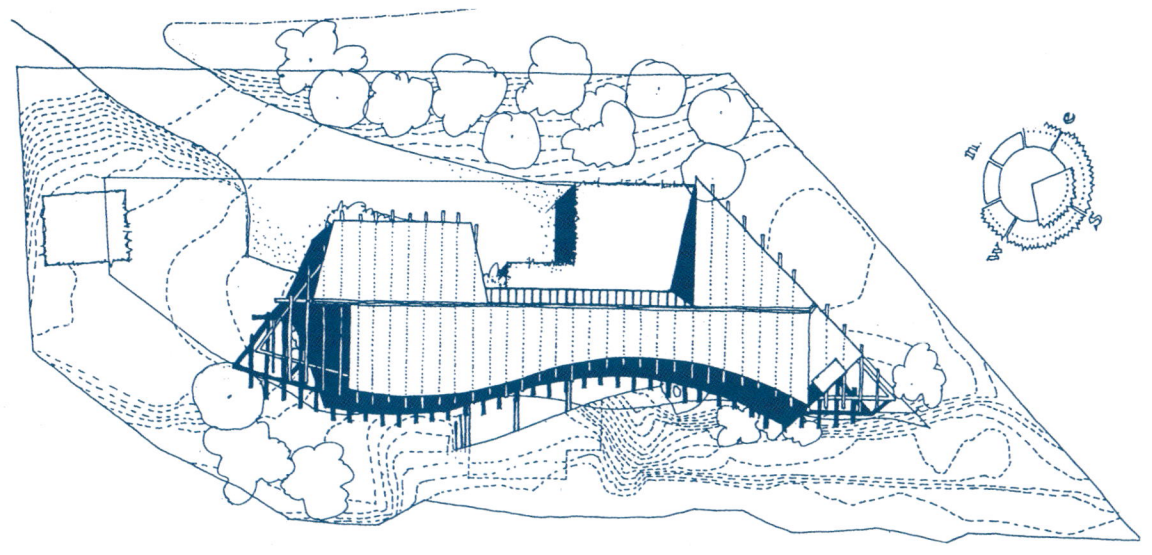
Site plan

Playa Escondida House

Playa Escondida, Lima, Peru

Photographs: Jean-Marie Monthiers

In the design of this dwelling the aim was to concentrate the interest on two architectural directions within the same spatial treatment: one opens the closed spaces, while the other closes the open spaces. These opposed conditions are unified by the dynamics of the vertical and horizontal planes. It is what their creators define as "the continuous movement of matter".

This dwelling consists of a cube whose base is a centripetal closed courtyard crossed by horizontal strata that emerge vertically over the high volume, with the transparency contained inside a continuous strip of concrete. This dynamic central space created a changing panorama inside the house. To prolong this idea, it was decided to cover the stairwell of glass bricks, black mosaic and of coloured tiles, creating a pictorial image and at the same time one of industrial perfection. These materials elegantly communicate an idea of coolness that is very appropriate for a beach dwelling. With the incorporation of a palm, the dwelling manages to take advantage of all its vertical drive, showing the presence of nature in an environment in which mineral elements are predominant. The dwelling is articulated around the courtyard, so that each side of the cube has its function, some protecting the interior and the others creating habitable spaces.

The ground floor houses the children's rooms and guest rooms, the service room, a utility room and a garage for a car and a boat. The upper floor houses the common living areas in a single space. This part of the dwelling is completely glazed and its double height is prolonged through a covered gallery that gives access to the narrow swimming pool. Above, suspended over this double height, is the main bedroom, a bathroom and a solarium facing the Pacific Ocean.

Section DD

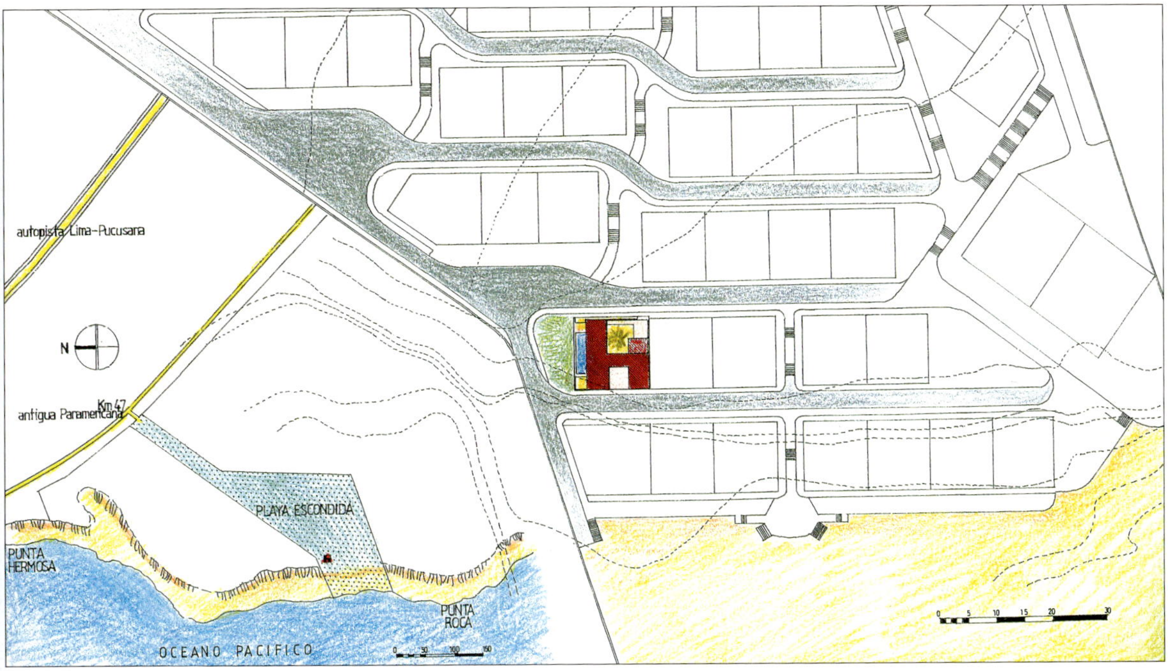
autopista Lima-Pucusana
N
Km 47
antigua Panamericana
PLAYA ESCONDIDA
PUNTA HERMOSA
PUNTA ROCA
OCEANO PACIFICO

Site plan

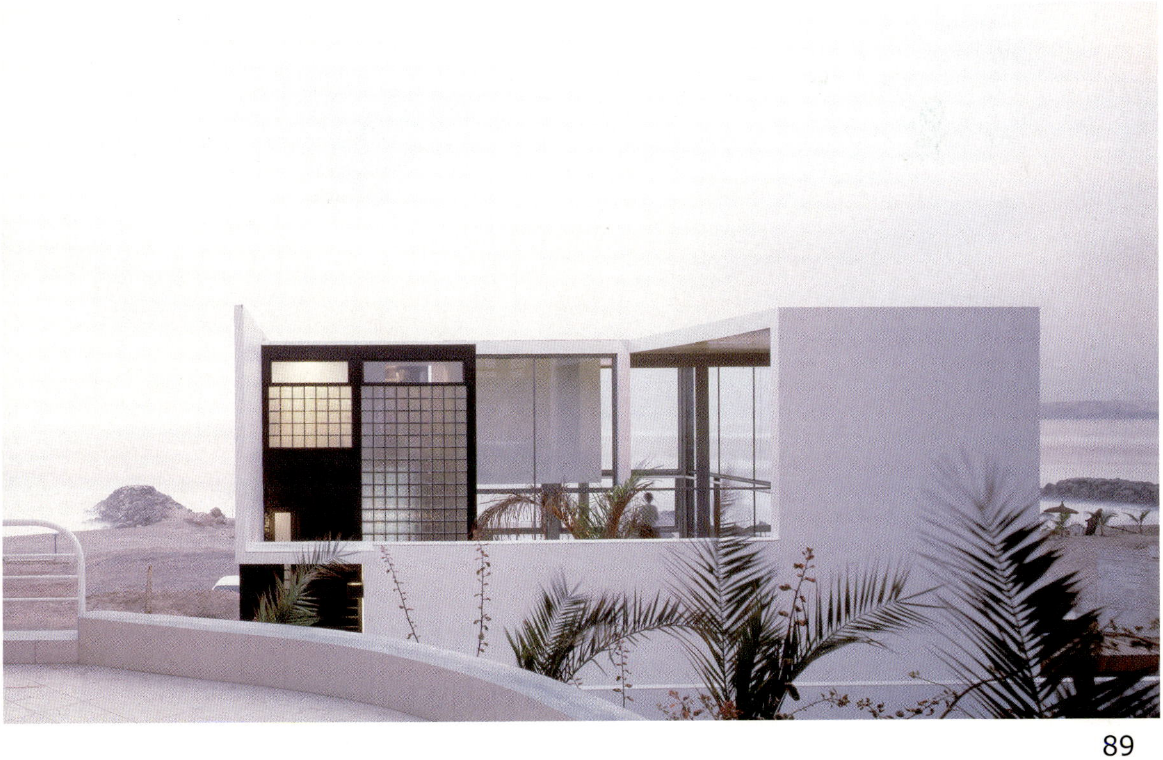

A completely glazed volume located right beside the pool and with a sea view serves as a support for the porch of the terrace, which acts as a frame for the whole scheme.

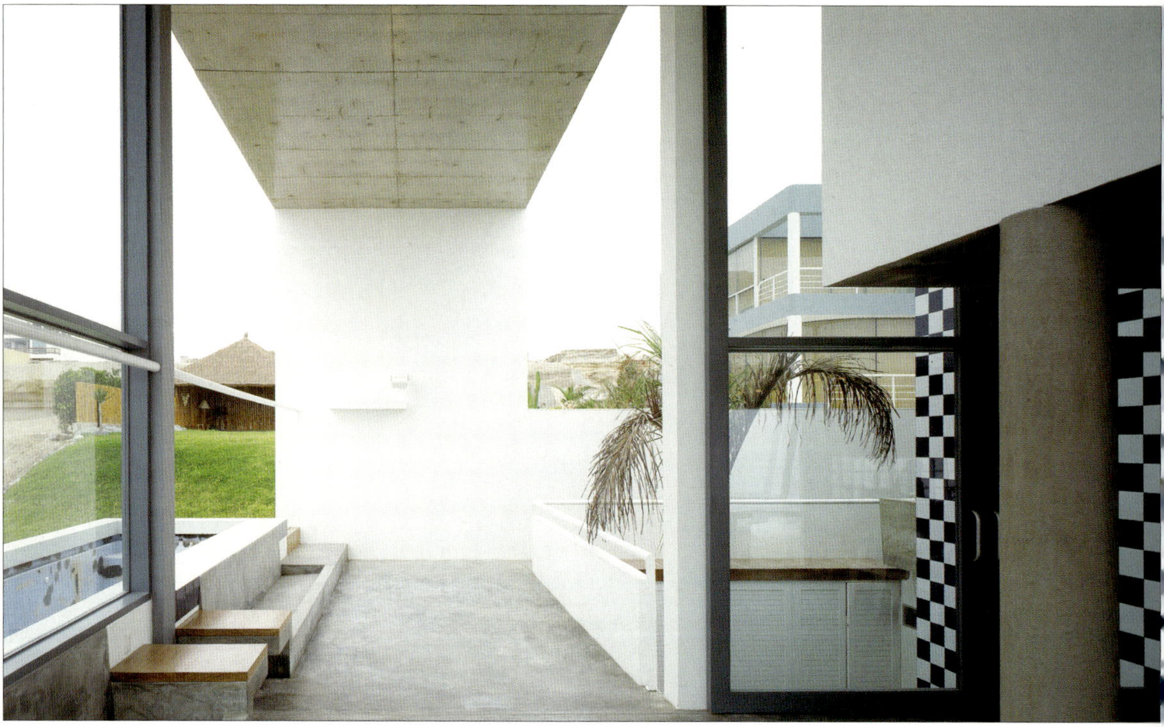

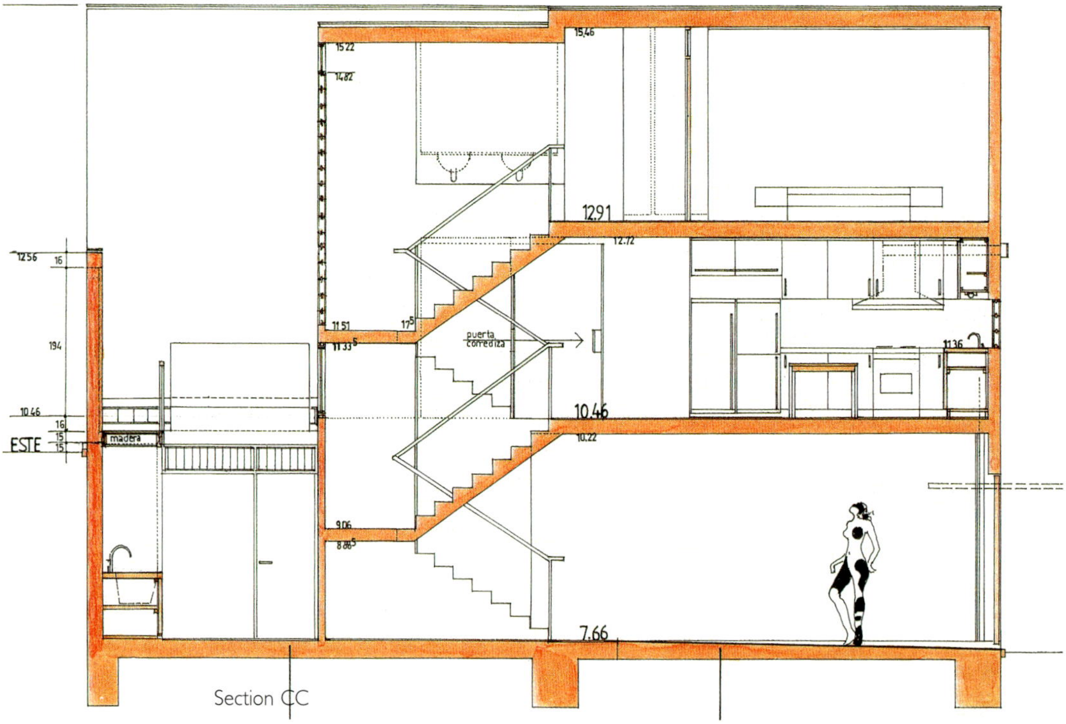
15.46
15.22
14.82
12.91
12.72
12.56
16
194
10.46
16
15
15
ESTE
madera
11.51
11.33
puerta corrediza
11.36
10.46
10.22
9.06
8.86
7.66

Section CC

Jackson Clements Burrows Pty Ltd Architects

Riverside Terrace

Victoria, Australia

Photographs: John Hay

Riverside Terrace is a suitable weekend residence for interacting with the environment, a place where one goes to meditate, to relax or to be liberated, where the experiences are associated with an environment of peace that affects the subconscious of its inhabitants. Although the dwelling establishes a rural aesthetics in the environment of a beach, on the banks of the river Barwon in Victoria, Australia, the fundamental aim in the design was the desire to create a house that was directly associated with the medium in which it was located, starting from the premise that the interior and exterior architecture must be considered as one. The external use of materials characteristic of the interior removed the distinction between the interior spaces and the garden.

The design of the building makes use of a cross-flow of ventilation due to its limited width and to the design of devices like the double folding doors and the blinds on the windows that allow the ventilation to be controlled in the whole house. The large west windows are protected by mobile external screens that provide shade, thus reducing the impact of the evening sun. The external awnings located in front of the living room create pleasant shaded spaces for the hot summer months, while in winter they can be raised to increase the penetration of sunlight.

The main priorities of the project were privacy, interrupted views and an architectural aesthetics that naturally determined an alternative lifestyle, separated from the regularity and order of cosmopolitan life. The internal layout is determined by an association of protective spaces that conceal the interior of the adjacent properties. The main area includes the living room, the dining room and the kitchen, forming a whole that opens up to expand the views of the river. As a result, the architectural form is based on the depth of the scheme and leads the visual focus toward the material form, the axis of the river and the interior spaces. Finally, the building was designed for flexible use, so that it could be adapted to the number of occupants and the length of stay. The occupants can thus open the house more or less according to their needs.

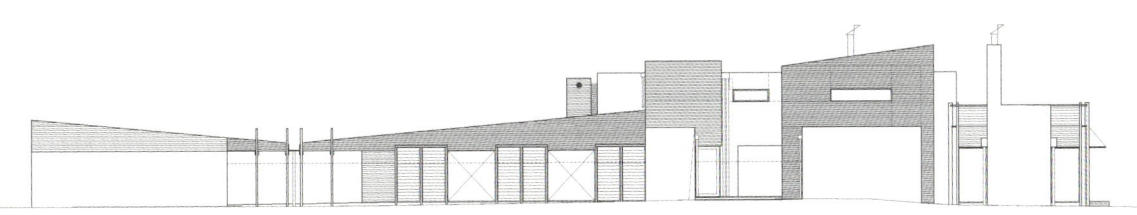

South elevation

A terrace of rational lines and with a finish that recalls that of boats serves as a meeting point on the exterior of the building. This space has excellent views over the river, and its design and functionality make it one of the key architectural elements in this house.

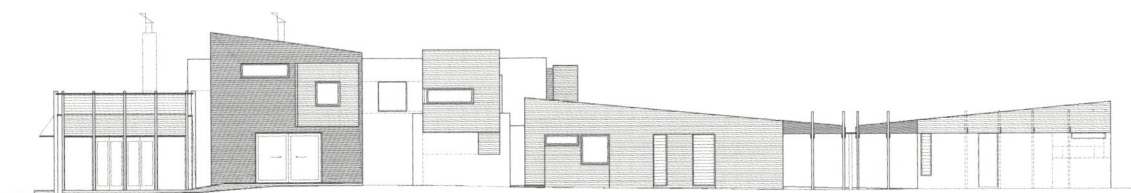

North elevation

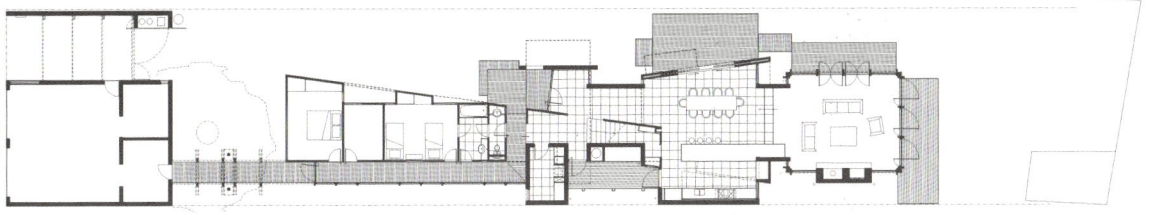

Grounf floor plan

Sliding doors help to create transparent spaces. This system and the mixed use of materials such as different-coloured wood help to erase the distinction between interior and exterior.

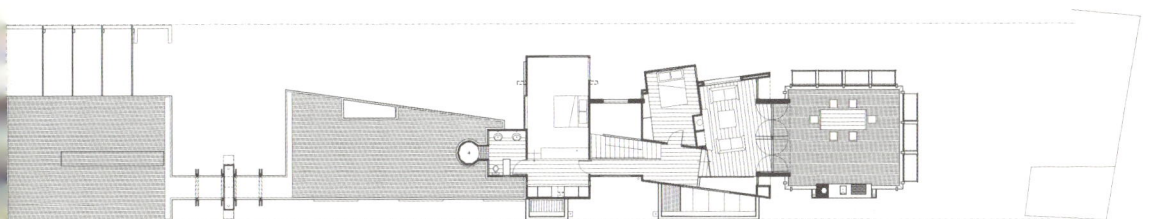

First floor plan

Jarmund / Vigsnæs AS Architects MNAL
Summer Cabin on the Coast of Norway
Norway

Photographs: Nils Petter Dale

This dwelling is sited on the south coast of Norway, a perfect aquatic landscape in which it seemed difficult to build without altering its balanced nature. The solution devised for this scheme was an attempt to strengthen the line between the different natural spaces, thus reinforcing the understanding between the parts and the transition between them.

This building replaces an old cabin that was demolished. It is a dwelling that serves as a barrier between the beach and the oak forest, which becomes a secluded garden.

The building was structured in such a way that two large doors facing each other open the space and create a cross movement, allowing the contact between the rooms to be controlled through the main room of the dwelling. In counterpoint to these large openings that oxygenate the interior and fill it with light, the rest of the house is relatively closed. The windows were set in frames that stand out from the sloping walls of the dwelling, with an inclination contrary to that of the facades, in which some of the panels have been left exposed. The conceptual configuration of the sloping external walls was established in order to gain light and to give a certain movement to the structure. The incorporation of another small building a few meters from the end of the dwelling —a warehouse with a butterfly roof— creates a slight break with the order established by the main building, which has a gable roof. The panels that cause the inclination of the facades are made of oak, a material that is tough and durable, fits into the landscape and recalls the old marine constructions in the area. In the interior, the floors of slate and painted wooden combine with the decorative elements, which were specially designed for this new "cabin".

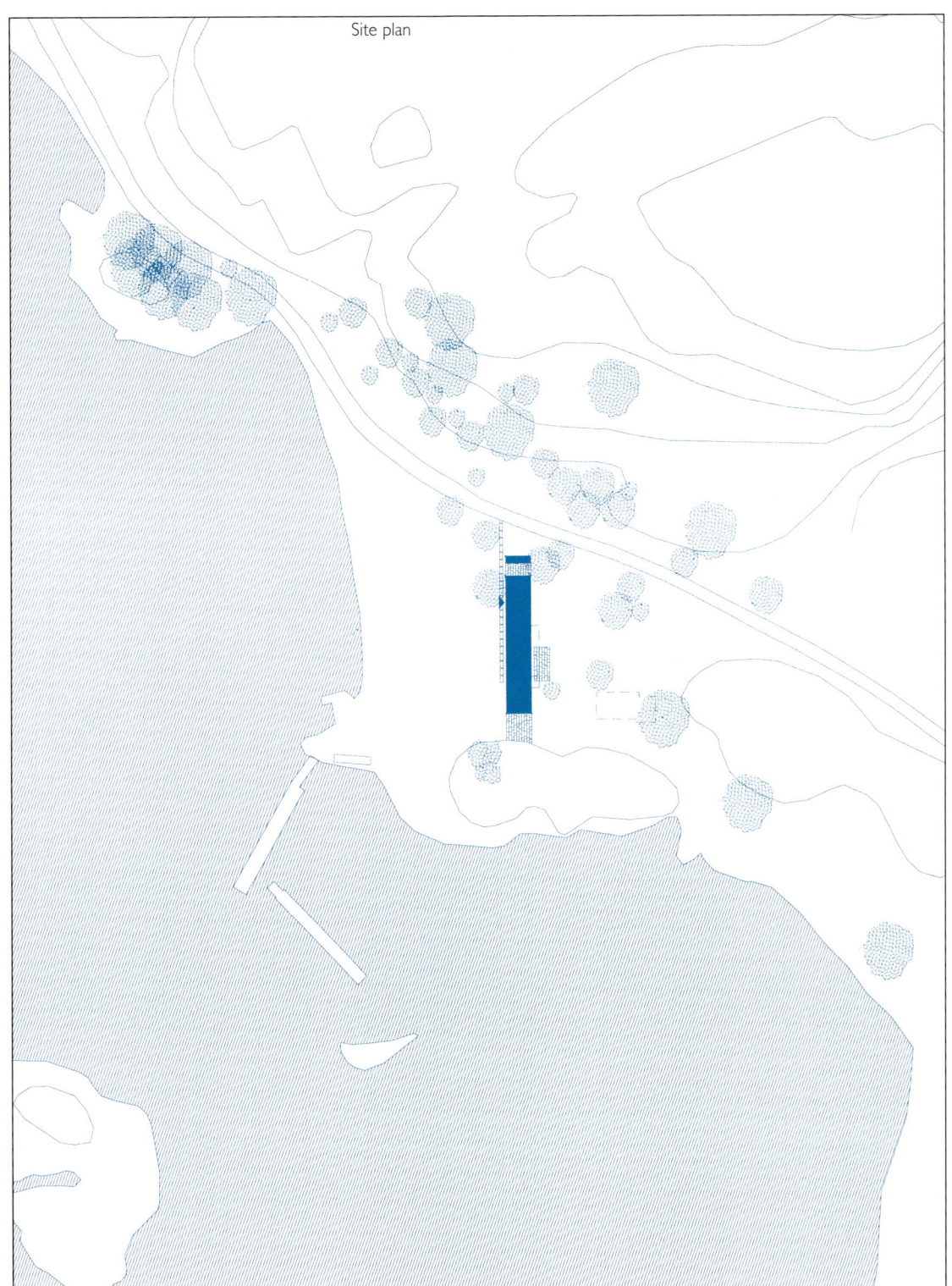
Site plan

The composition of the different planes of the dwelling, with facades and windows sloping in opposite directions, the choice of materials and the incorporation of a second body with a butterfly roof give great personality to this project.

Jordi Garcés
House in Costa Brava
Sant Feliu de Guixols, Spain

Photographs: Lluís Casals

This holiday house is situated 95 m above the sea at a spectacular point of the Costa Brava, a privileged position with unique views. The building and its inhabitants immediately establish a close relationship with the Mediterranean and the sky, with the permanent presence of the coastline discreetly in the background.

In the design of this 450 sqm dwelling, the topographical difficulties of the site were overcome through the creation of a large plane housing the main leisure areas: the living room, the dining room, the kitchen, the access courtyard, the terraces and the swimming pool. Below, the bedrooms are sheltered by the bottom surface of this plane, in a more private situation but with access to the exterior.

A line perpendicular to the sea crosses the building from one end to another, giving unity to the whole. It runs from earth to sea, starting from the lower courtyard. A shady porch extends towards the pool, a visible volume of water whose central sector connects with the two levels of the double interior space.

The materials chosen by the architect were render and paint on the walls, metal frames and tiled floors in the courtyards to establish a continuity with the interiors, and wood for the terraces. Finally, the roof design consisted of a central area of conventional Arab tiles surrounded by a peripheral copper channel.

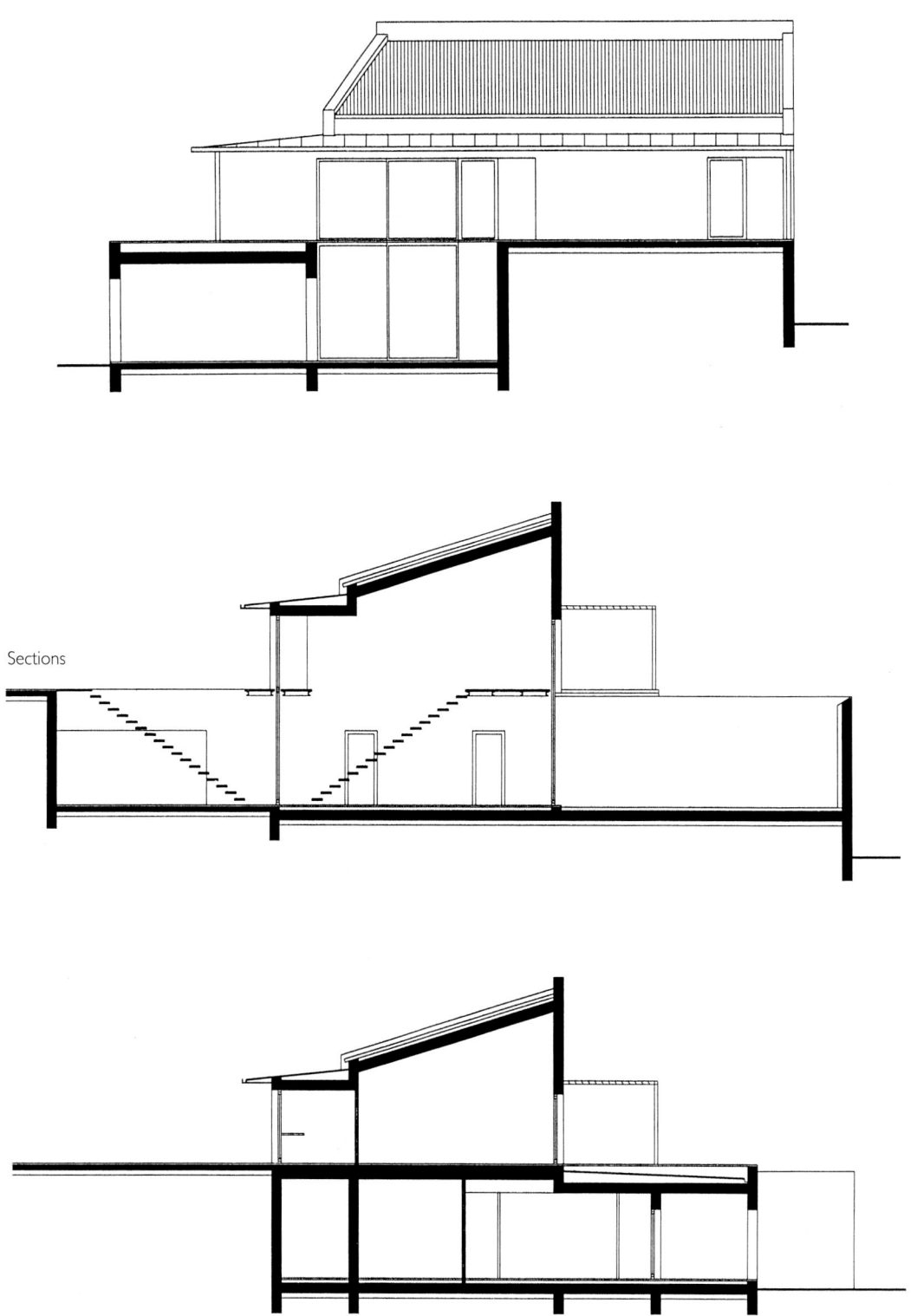

Sections

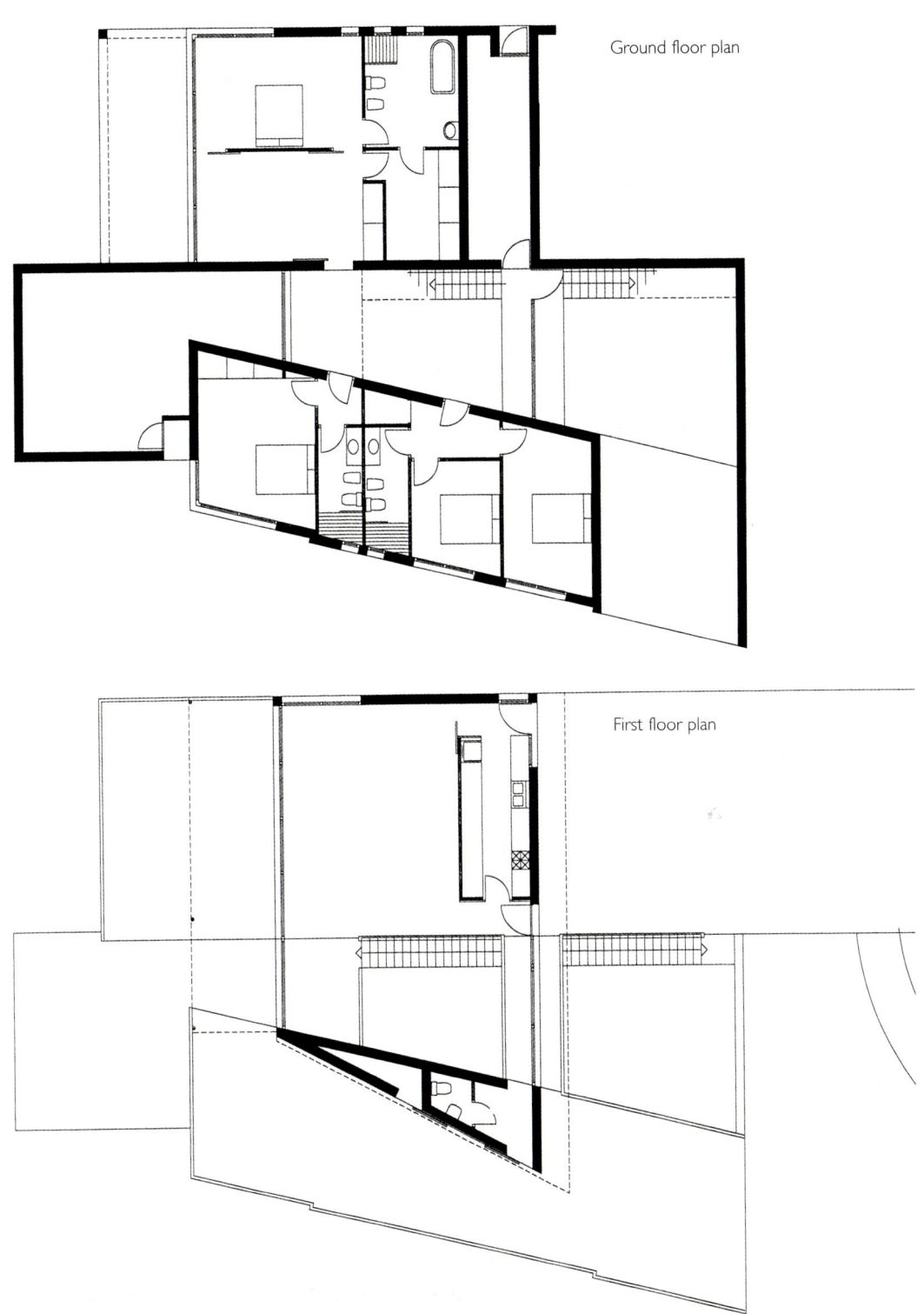

In the layout of this dwelling the architect took into account the topographical characteristics of the location. The different levels serve as specific areas, and the more sheltered areas were reserved for the bedrooms.

In the interior spaces, the natural light coming through the glazed doors and the windows fills all the spaces and surfaces with colour. The transparency of one of the walls of the living room allows the pool to form part of the interior design, which also features a staircase with cantilevered steps.

José Cruz Ovalle
House in Santo Domingo
Rocas de Santo Domingo, Chile

Photographs: Juan Purcell

This dwelling located on a slope facing the sea is raised above the land on reinforced concrete slabs and built entirely in wood, thus providing an effective and aesthetic solution to the problem of damp that is often found in coastal areas.

In this building of 350 sqm on a plot of 1,135 sqm the architects attempted to configure a space "illuminated" by the surrounding landscape and not simply dominated by it, as often happens in houses located on the seafront. The seascape usually steals the interior space by dissipating it toward the horizon in a single direction. To respond to this presence, the architects invented the "counter-view", which seeks its power in the maximum expansion of a space that opens its depth in multiple directions. This is achieved by rotating the house around a courtyard that is open to the sea and sheltered from the prevailing winds, in order to form a double interior. This rotation partly accommodates the slope of the land by means of the different horizontal levels of the floor, as a way of multiplying the vertical lines in order to create the oblique depths that measure and graduate the characteristic "up" and "down" relationship of a sloping site.

The "counterview" is thus here the abstraction that proposes an oriented but not directed interior and that balances the eloquence of the landscape by means of a space developed in different directions that relates proximity and distance. This exercise allows the surrounding dual elements (the land and its slope, the neighbouring houses and their gardens, the extension of the beach and the reef, the distance of the sea and the horizon...) to illuminate the interior of this house without dominating it.

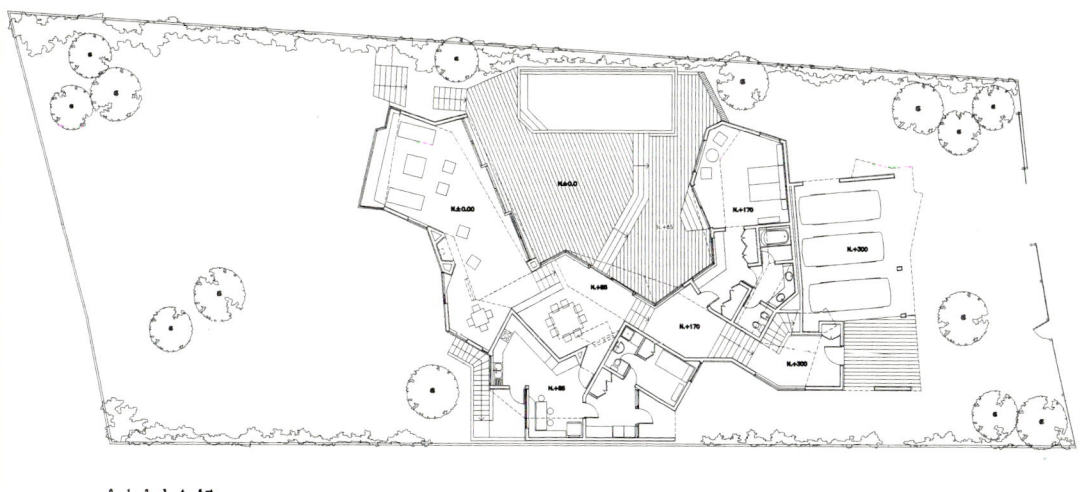

Ground floor plan

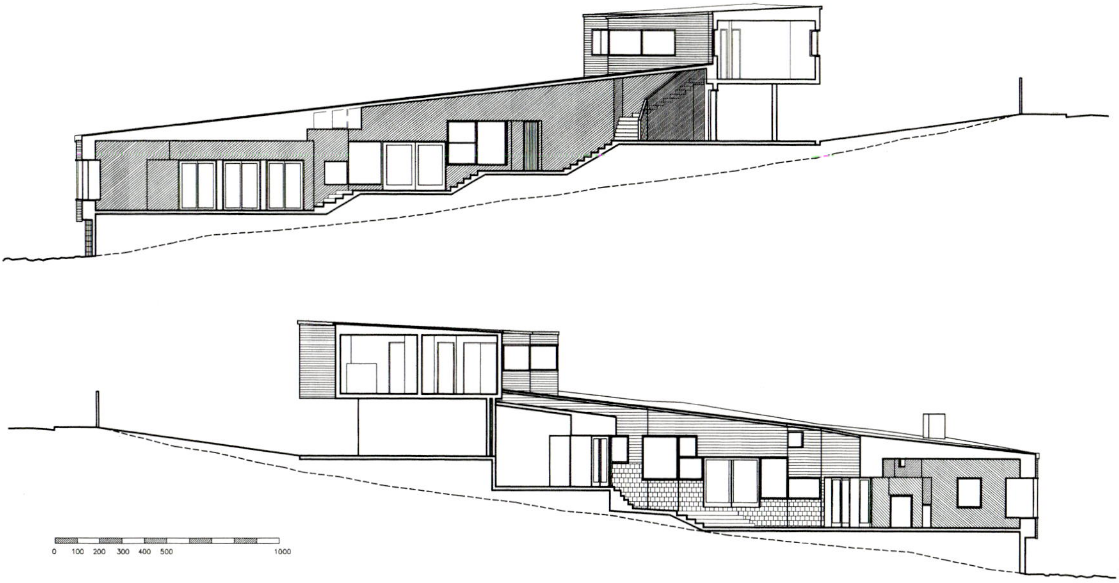

Cross section

Josep Lluís Mateo & Arturo Vila
House in Artà
Mallorca, Spain

Photographs: Duccio Malagamba

This single-family dwelling is located in an area of the Majorcan coast that has not been developed previously due to the harsh north winds, the oppressive heat and the distance from more inhabited areas.

The house moves with these forces of nature: it protects itself from the wind, it generates natural ventilation in its interior to regulate the temperature in summer, and it has a small courtyard with a controlled microclimate. However, at the same time it opens up to the exterior, in a spectacular display of nature and its energy.

Volumetrically the house is almost entirely crystalline, though it also has a mineral tone that is very appropriate because it is set very close to the rocky massif of Mont Farrutx. The predominant geometry of the composition is based on cubes of different sizes that present a different face on each of their sides but with a common denominator: apertures that open it to varying degrees to the exterior and contribute to the ventilation. As a result, this interplay of volumes allows the dwelling to adapt perfectly to different situations and uses, thus creating both private and more extroverted spaces. It is distributed on three levels: basement, ground floor and first floor, and is articulated through the central structure of the main volume, to which three smaller volumes are added. On the ground floor, the main volume houses the living room and the interior dining room. On the first floor are the bedrooms and the guest wing, overhanging the garden and separated by a small courtyard that provides light to the ground floor. The first of the attached volumes houses the access, the staircase and the study on the first floor; the second houses the kitchen; and between them a metal volume contains the bathroom of the upper level and offers shelter for the courtyard over which it is placed. Finally, the basement houses the garage and the technical facilities.

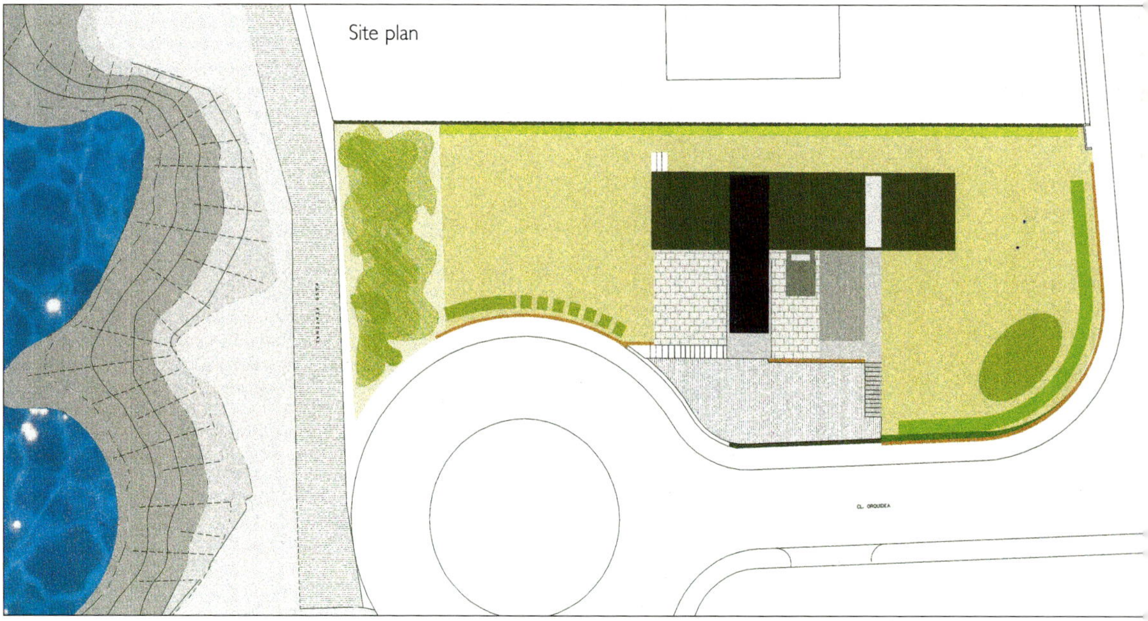

Site plan

The dwelling is articulated as a series of interlocking cubes. The use of different colours and materials on their exterior helps to highlight the presence of these volumes.

Elevation

The ground floor is complemented by an inner courtyard used as a summer dining room and the kitchen, with white furniture and work areas (kitchen and sink) in a metal island.

Legorreta + Legorreta
House La Cruz
El Tamarindo, Jalisco. Mexico

Photographs: Lourdes Legorreta

El Tamarindo is one of those places where the sea and the woods cohabit naturally, forming a suitable setting for a dwelling in which one can enjoy nature in all its glory.

The main house is located at the top of a hill, while the pool and a guest room are on two smaller mounds. The central theme of the house was the cross, a sign with deep historical meanings in almost all cultures that also allowed the architects to take advantage of the different views, to provide cross ventilation in all the spaces and to adapt the building to the land whilst doing the least damage to the trees. At the centre of the cross is a lobby that unites the different spaces and levels of the house and leads to a belvedere located on the third floor. In each arm the main elements of the house were located, always seeking an intimate relationship with nature and with the surrounding trees. This theme was continued in the form of the pool and in the design of the furniture, crockery, doors, bed linen, towels, and even the stationery.

Each room has a different personality. The main room is located on a lower level and is closely related to the vegetation, while in the two rooms on the upper floor the design of the wooden ceilings became the main theme. The cylindrical guest bungalow was built separately from the main house and is very independent. The house is thus designed as an architectural space that favours the creation of different atmospheres.

To take advantage of the external spaces, a hammock area and belvedere offer 360° views of the Tamarind forest. The dwelling is communicated with the pool by a wooden walkway that goes through the wood from one building to the other —yet another proof of the determination to create an architecture that was committed to the landscape, in which the volumes are integrated with nature and with the climate.

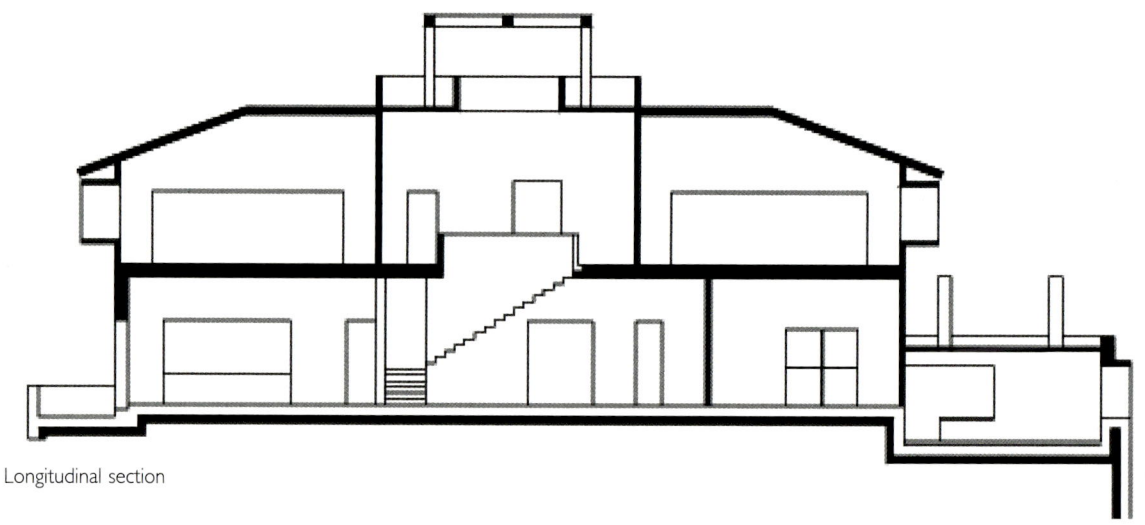

Longitudinal section

The use of wood and warm colours in most of the interior spaces helps to create a peaceful, sophisticated atmosphere. In contrast, the windows that open onto the green landscape provide light and coolness in the rooms.

MVRDV
Borneo Houses
Amsterdam, The Netherlands

Photographs: Nicholas Kane

In Borneo (Sporenburg) two dwellings stand out because of their resolution and the great spatial possibilities applied inside their limited size.

The first of the dwellings, located on plot 18, is 4.2 metres wide and 16 metres high and has a spacious terrace of double height in the facade giving onto the sea. Initially the regulations only allowed the construction of three floors, a high floor at street level and two more above it. Despite this, the architects were able to build four floors by building in blocks and setting one of the four levels at the rear. A long traverse section was also designed with two "closed" elements: a space with direct access to the street that serves as a garage, and another block suspended over the terrace and the water on the second level that stands out from the rest of the building and houses the bedroom and a bathroom. The remaining irregular space of the house — the kitchen-dining room, the living room and the study— are communicated so as to provide a fluid and simple transition from one room to the next. The rooms were designed with different heights and degrees of privacy. Each one is directly connected to the exterior through an exclusive access, with the double height terrace, an overhanging window and a roof garden aligned in the rear facade.

On plot 12 a very unusual private dwelling was designed in an experiment to adapt the distribution to the narrow site. Due to this restriction and to the fact that only half of the width was used, the result is an alley and the narrowest house imaginable —only 2.5 metres wide. Breaking with normal practice, the whole length and height of the half that was built along the back street has a glass facade, while the facades that give onto the street and the channel were left entirely closed. This open facade rotates the house to face the alley, so that the exterior and interior are presented as a single space. The alley accommodates three differentiated elements: a block that serves for storage whose roof slopes towards the street providing a parking space, and two closed volumes, a block containing a guest room and bathroom, and a block that provides additional width to the studios on the first and second floor. These last two volumes are suspended in the glass facade, containing the exterior space and giving life to the alley. An extremely narrow house thus became a sufficiently spacious dwelling.

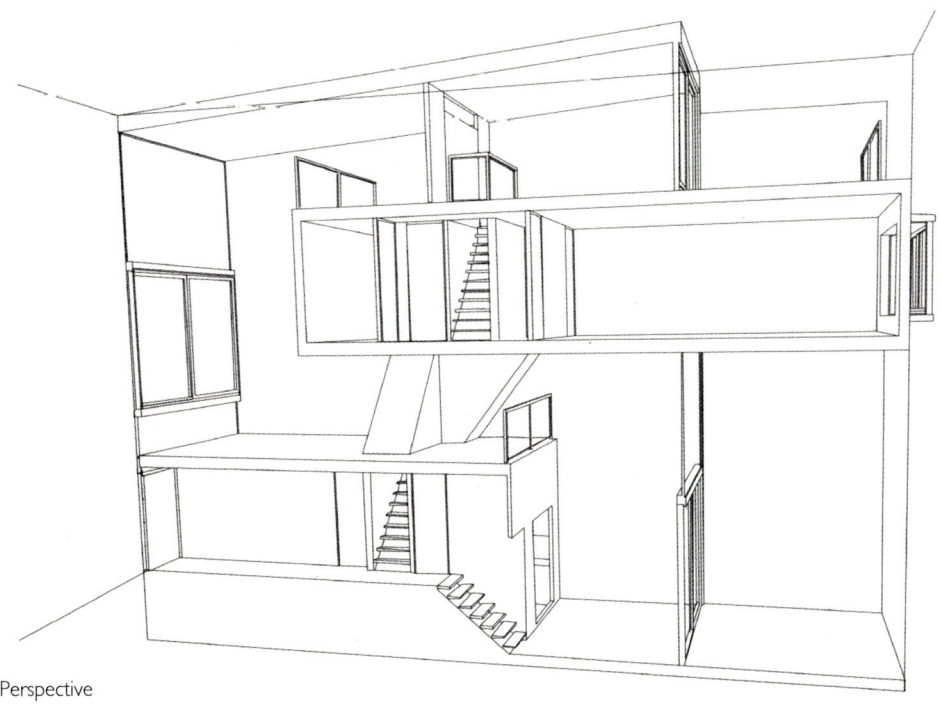
Perspective

The use of displaced volumes gives this dwelling large, double-height space, half of which is a covered terrace looking onto the canal.

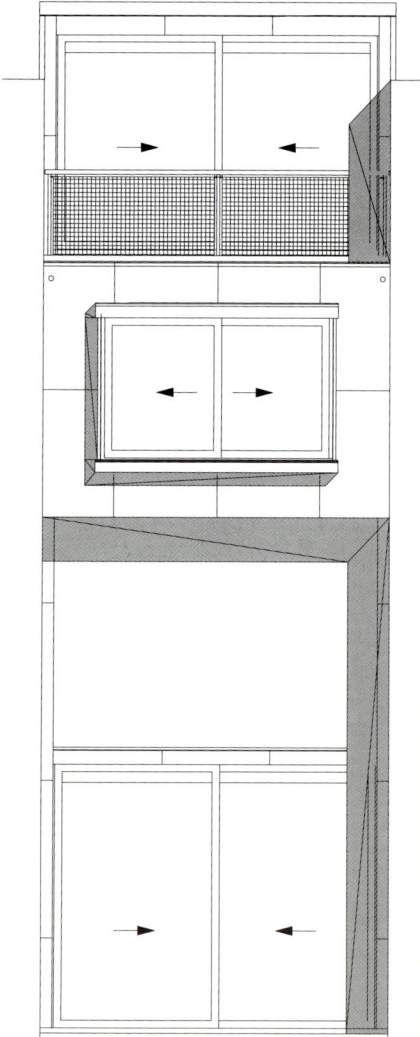

Elevation waterside

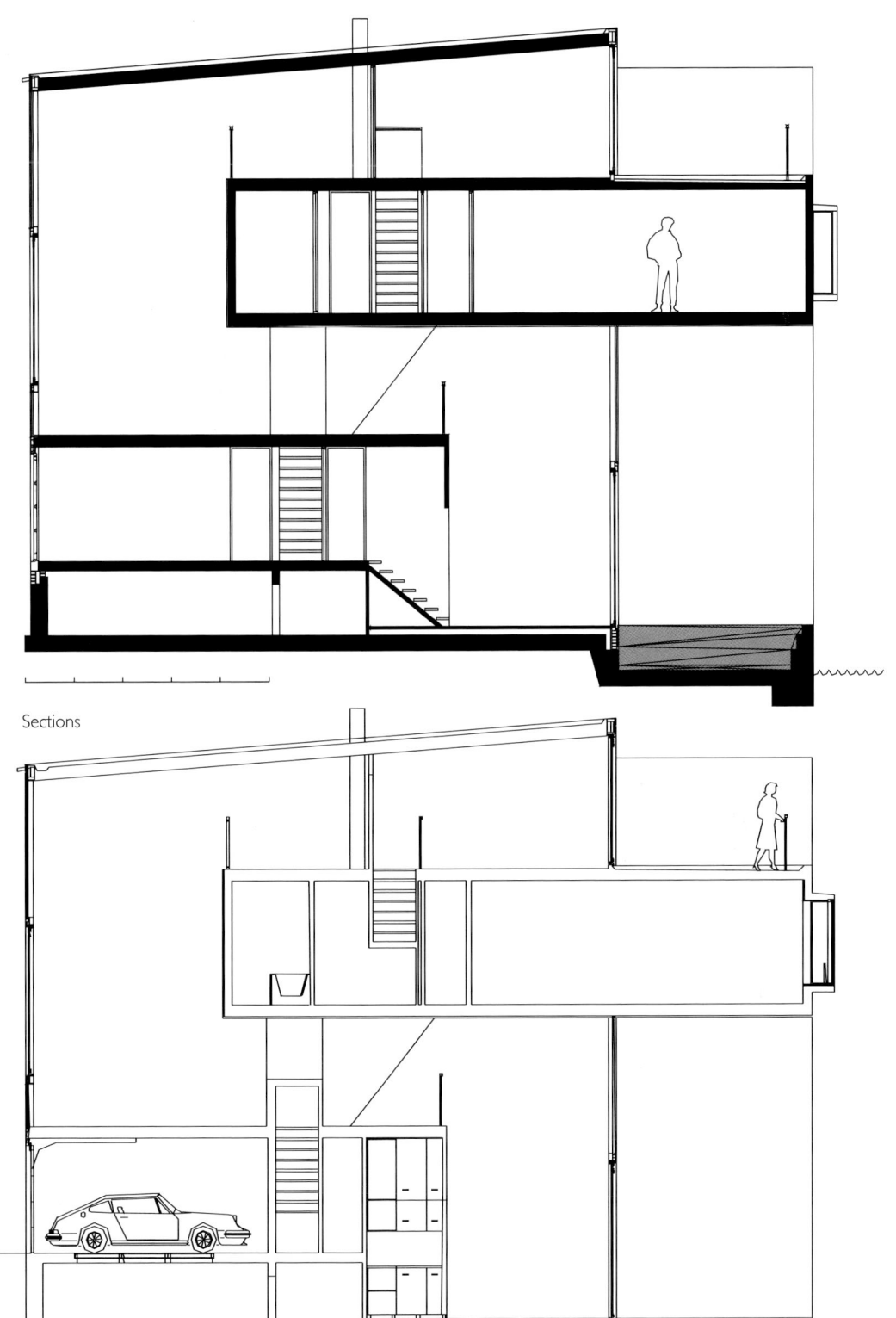

Sections

Plot 12

Unlike the neighbouring dwellings, because the site was so narrow this house has its fully glazed main facade at the side facing the alley. Modules were added to enlarge the building and give it personality.

Elevation waterside

Niall McLaughlin
Northamptonshire Shack
Northamptonshire, UK

Photographs: Nicholas Kane

This dwelling is located on agricultural land that was used as a reconnaissance base by the allied forces during the Second World War. The building was constructed manually, without any working drawings and in conjunction with a landscape scheme, so in its development the modifications were open to all those involved. The client, a photographer specialised in insects and elements of nature with back lighting and special effects, wanted a house that also served as a setting for his work. He therefore decided to regenerate an abandoned pond that was lost between a labyrinth of brambles and bushes. After the water had been filtered and oxygenated with plants, the brambles and bushes had been cleared away and the water had been populated with fish, the pond recovered its life and could attract the dragonflies and other animals that would be used as models for the photographer. The form and the materials of the building were conceived with the intention of capturing and storing several types of light. Some external spaces, such as the south area giving onto the pond, are used as rooms in which objects could be placed for photographing under the required conditions. A long arm was also built over the pond to photograph insects on the surface with the water as a background. To take advantage of the geographical situation of this dwelling, the architect incorporated a sauna, a bedroom and a belvedere with views over the aquatic landscape and the surrounding grasslands.

The building combines wood, masonry, metal cladding and other elements, and a glass-fibre wing whose extended staircases of polycarbonate and perforated metal emerge from the water. Due to the curious external appearance the access to the dwelling is like the entrance to a hidden cave. The main elements of the structure are the numerous "wing" elements that crawl over the rear part of the building, the skylight that runs along the longitudinal axis and a complex overhanging roof supported by fine metal angles laid out in a fan-shape that bend with the force of the strong wind that blows in this area.

Perspective

floor plan

181

Pete Bossley
House in Bay of Islands
Bay of Islands, New Zealand

Photographs: Patrick Reynolds

This house is in a beautiful private bay, at the foot of a hill covered with thick vegetation in Bay of Islands, one of the places with the best climate in New Zealand. Unlike most houses that have been built in the bays, where the colonial tradition tends to be predominant, this three-bedroom holiday house is discreetly concealed between the trees that surround it. The dwelling has a "sleepout" for sleeping outdoors on hot summer nights and a boatshed. The house and sleepout are a demonstration of the enthusiasm that Bossley feels for the transparencies of Modernism and for the wooden buildings that have been developed by New Zealand architects since the fifties.

In this building glass is the main feature, and the two main facades are like large cabinets that open up unashamedly toward the landscape. The depth thus expands and contracts as if it were determined by the requirements of the rooms. Each room has maximum exposure, both to the exterior with the beach and the sea on the east side, and through the peaceful corridor toward the forest and the evening sun in the west. The views, the sun, the natural ventilation and the external spaces protected from the cool sea breezes were the elements that were analysed with most attention, and they all follow the same linear plane that gives shape to this project. This linear plane follows a north-south axis, meeting the sloping terrain on eight different levels, so that the dwelling is like a large staircase in which each step is a different room. Also, each level is clearly defined by the structural frames, since the walls were left free of any structural function.

The shed roof gets wider as it falls towards the lower level and provides up to three metres of shade on the wooden terraces of each room. It is 40 metres long, suspended on the walls, and supported on a laminated wood frame.

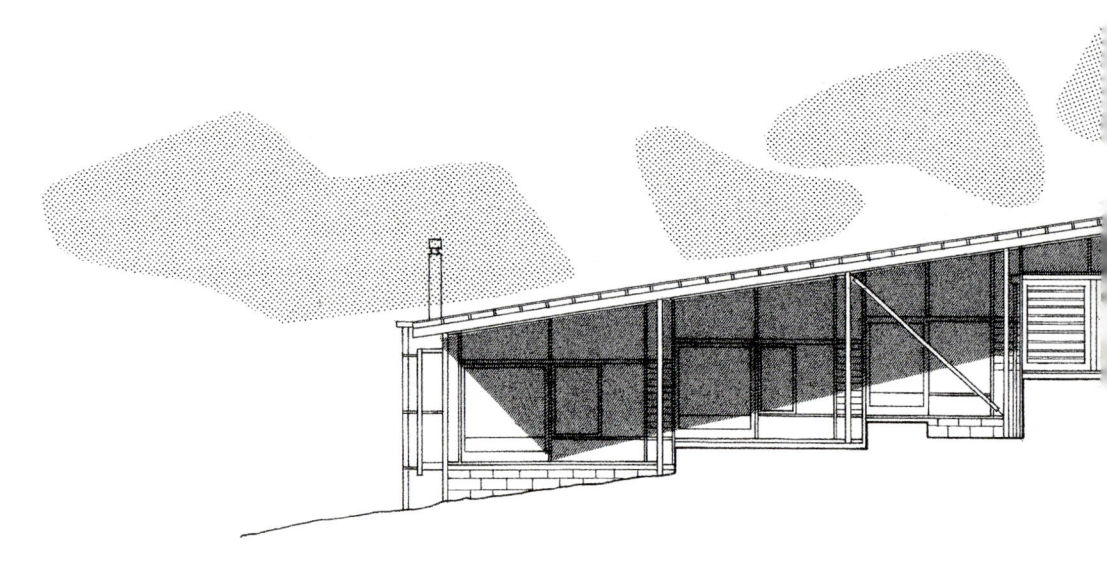

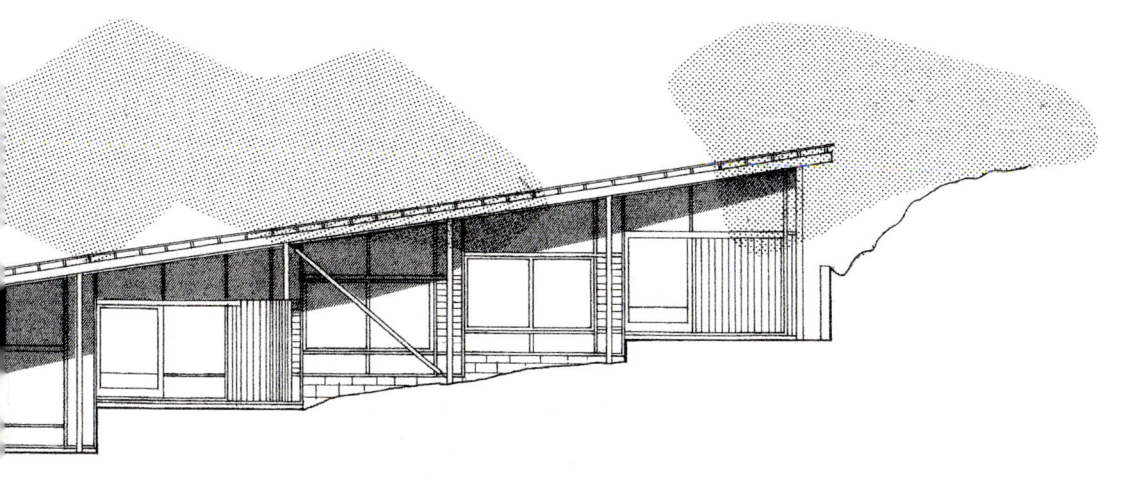
West elevation

Philip Gumuchdjian
D.P. Think Tank / Boathouse

Skibbereen, Country Cork, Ireland

Photographs: W. Hutchmacher / ARTUR

Set into the River Ilen in west Ireland, the building was conceived as a retreat for a famous film producer.

The architecture reflect a wide range of references: boathouse structures, barns, cow sheds, chlets, and a European perspective on Japanese pavilions. The building resolves these references into a simple expression of frame, rof and screens.

The dominant element of the design is the overhanging roof structure wich provides physical and psychological protection from the considerable annual rainfall.

A clear hierarchy of architectral elements (roof, structure, screens and glazing) was crucial to creating its legibility as an apparently enclosed "found" structure —a simple and timeless object. Transparency and perforated screens were deployed to keep the building open to the elements but also frame views and suggest enclosure and protection.

The materials of the structure are selected to juxtapose "stable" elements such as glass and stainless steel against the highly "changeable" and weathering materials of the cedar roof planks, slats and decks and the iroko frame. Set against the vivid colours and reflections of the site —green fields, blue/silver river, dramatic blues and greys of the sky— the silver of the building permanently changes colour as roof and structural frame become wet during showers and bleached under the sunshine.

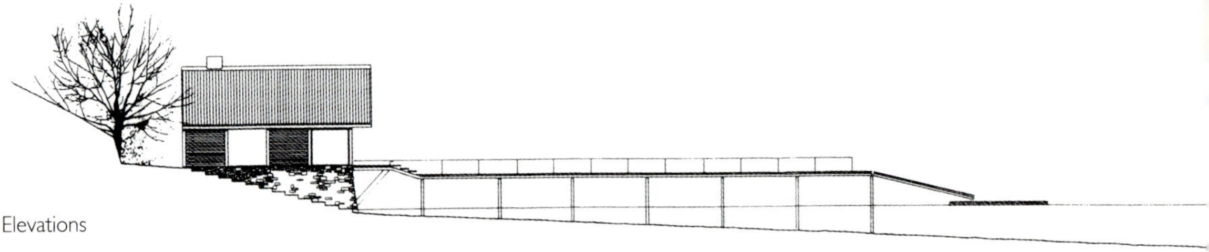

Elevations

Sketch

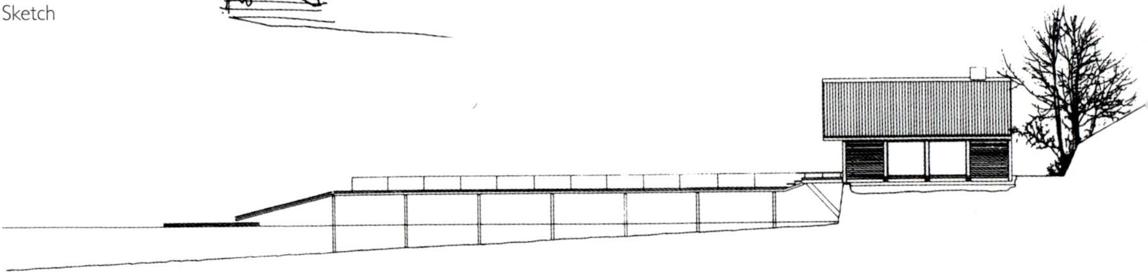

A long pier extends the house onto the river, creating a space for escape and a perspective from which the interior of the dwelling can be appreciated.

Richard Francis-Jones
Two houses in Woy Woy
Woy Woy, Australia

Photographs: Brett Boardman

The west banks of the waters of Brisbane, eighty kilometres to the north of Sydney, have a wide area of plains, a public reserve that connects in the north with the city Woy Woy. The side facing the land of this reserve is formed by a series of rows of houses made of wood and brick, so this space of linear architecture is an ideal place for the social life of the local community.

In this row of houses the architect Richard Francis-Jones conceived two new dwellings as the intersection of two basic forms: a rear courtyard surrounded with red brick walls that contains the land, protecting it and defining it; and an elegant wooden box that is totally open at one end and is built so that it is suspended on its foundations and displaced from the axis of the courtyard, seeking a seaward aspect. These two hollow forms one connected to the land and the other facing the sea were united and interlinked to create a space that formed the new dwellings. Although seemingly the forms are autonomous and the volumes are consistently articulated, they cross and overlap each other to give a reading in tune with the character of the place. Thus, the forms of the courtyard walled with clay bricks form a more intimate exterior/interior space in which the area of intersection with the houses is reserved for the kitchen and the utility areas. In turn, the wooden volume forms a kind of suspended jetty that opens onto the reserve and the port area. This main volume houses a spacious living room of double height, around which the bedrooms are arranged on the upper floor.

Finally, the precision of the construction and the geometry of its forms using natural, simple and economical materials is the origin of the poetic expression of this project.

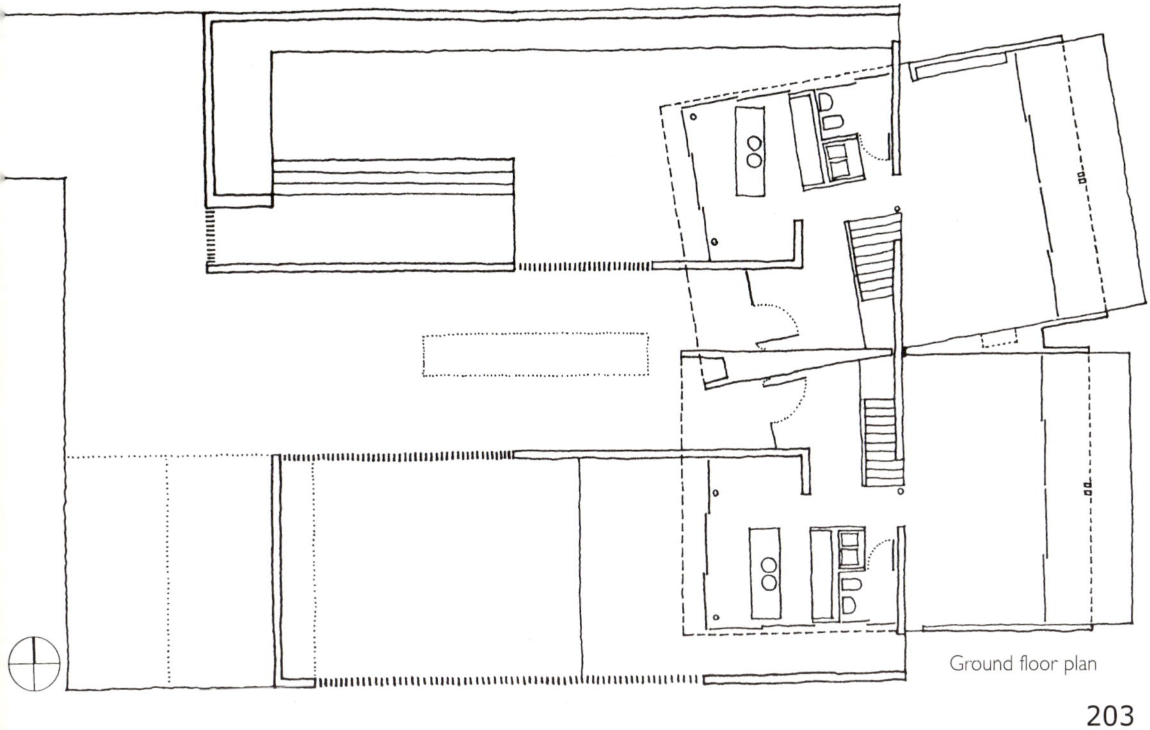

Ground floor plan

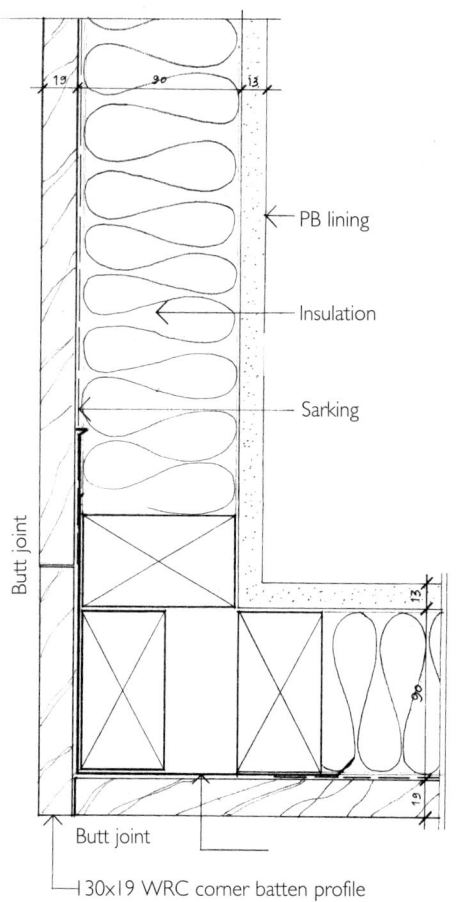

Typical west corner plan

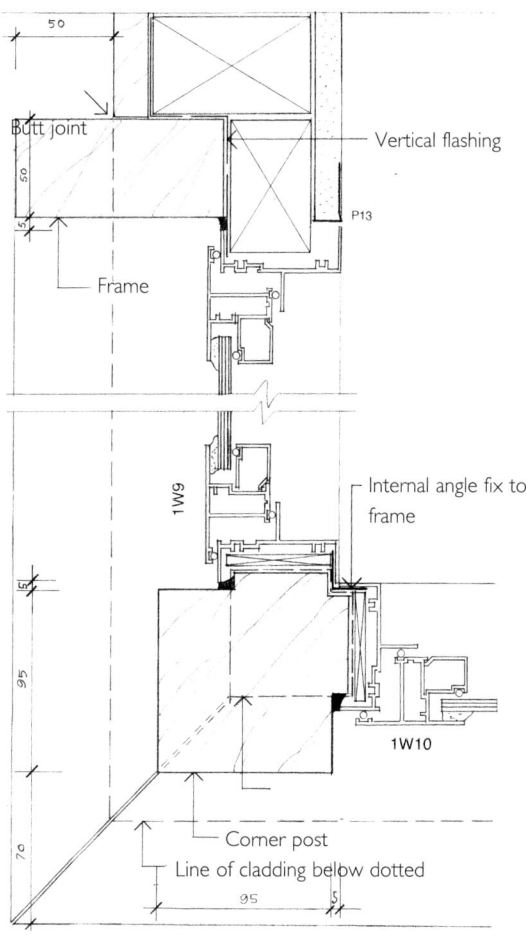

Typical west corner window plan

208

Sandra Barclay & Jean-Pierre Crousse
House B
Playa La Escondida, Cañete. Peru

Photographs: J.P.C. Photos

This project emerged from a process of reflection on certain factors that its architects judged to be essential: the climatic conditions of the Peruvian coast, the characteristics of the coast in which the dwelling was to be located and the client's needs. Although the Peruvian coast is formed by one of the most arid deserts in the world, its climate is not extreme.

Building a house in the desert in front of the sea gave Barclay and Crousse the opportunity to make a completely permeable architecture in which the walls only served to highlight the landscape and provide sufficient privacy for habitation. To meet the requirements of their clients, who sought a dwelling in which their children had independent spaces, the project was conceived with a clear vertical separation of generations. The house is divided into three independent levels joined by an external staircase: the parents occupy the upper level and the children the lower level, and are separated by the "social level", a place of encounter between the two generations. The staircase is the main structuring element, uniting the different levels and connecting each one to the beach. The fact that the staircase is external shows the functional autonomy of each level, reveals the slope of the land and offers us a view framed toward the sea from the moment one goes through the front door, located in the roof-garage. Each level also has a specific complementary activity expressed in environments defined by the same wall, which relates them to the landscape in different ways. The more private terrace on the parents' level was designed as a solarium supported by the wall and forming a balcony looking onto the sea. On the children's level, the wall acts as a filter to diminish the brightness of the light, framing the island through a vertical hole. Finally, the social level is the centre of gravity of the house, a space of double height giving it the status of the main area of the house. It has a large terrace, conceived as a "summer living room", partially protected by a pergola supported by the wall. A horizontal hole encased in it frames the sea and the nearby island.

Site plan

The abstraction of the architectural composition links the work to the architectural and artistic expressions of the Precolumbian period and the Spanish colonial period of the Peruvian coast.

The setting on a hillside with a slope of almost 45 degrees allows it to have a single front open to the exterior. Therefore, in order to create different ways of relating to the landscape and of enriching the univocal view, it was decided to dissociate the walls

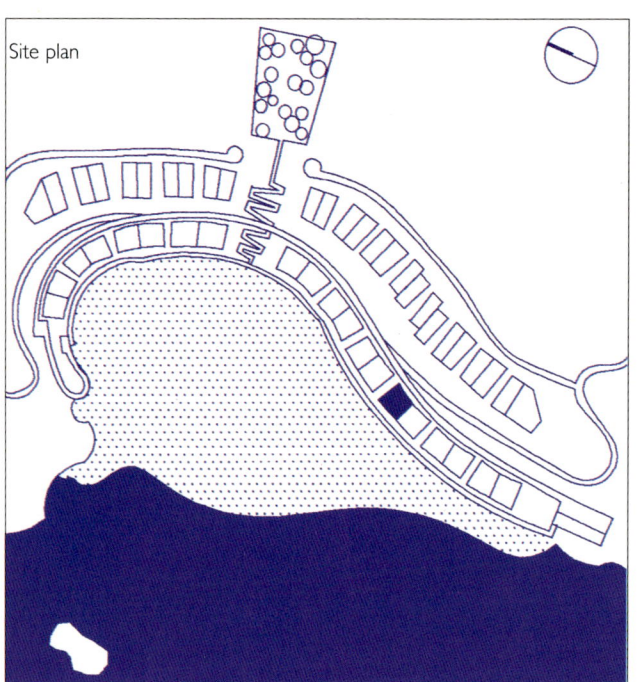

Section 4-4

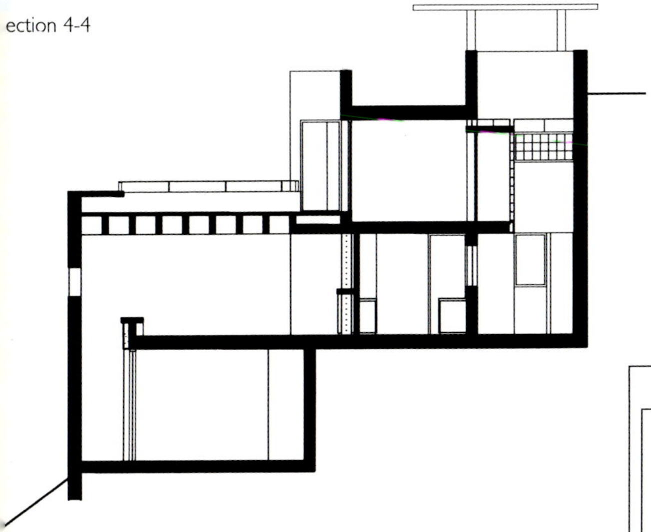

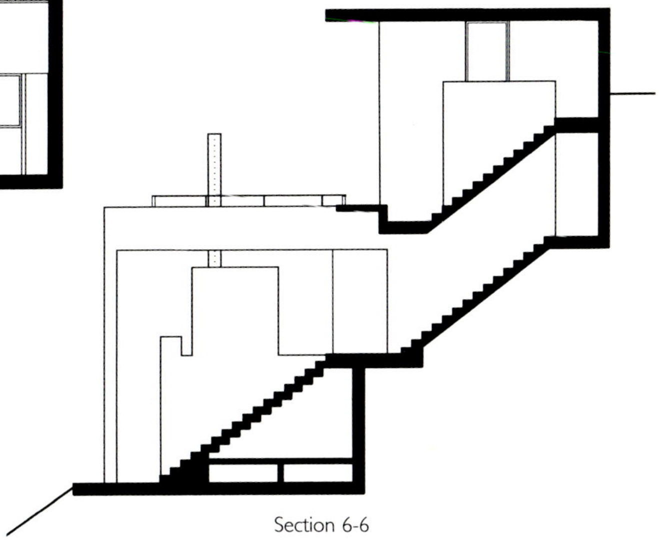

Section 6-6

215

The living room opens up toward the landscape. Light comes in through a source at the top of its double height and through the tempered glass screen that separates it from the terrace. The door has no frame and it is fully sliding, so the two spaces can be fully integrated to erase the limit between interior and exterior.

The access to the dwelling at the rear shows a large terrace with a porch that dominates the whole landscape.

Silvia Gmür & Livio Vacchini
3 Single–Family
Beinwil am See, Canton Argovia, Switzerland

Photographs: Vaclav Sedy

Located in the Swiss town of Beinwil am see these three single-family modules stand out from the architecture of the area due to their special design and arrangement. Three identical dwellings located on a hillside with a view of the lake give form to a single complex. The different modules share their foundations in kind of pedestal that determines part of their architectural character, enhancing their role in the landscape. The dwellings create a compositional rhythm in which the predominant geometry of the floors is the square, whereas in the elevations it is the rectangle. This rhythm is determined by a linear succession of "solids" and "voids" in which the former act as private spaces while the latter are used for the common living areas. The private space is divided in turn into porch and room, so the differentiation between exterior and interior is slightly blurred. The facades are composed of three differentiated elements that are used for their functionality and their aesthetic qualities: cement, glass and "air that in the void is converted into matter. It is an architecture that tends towards the essential without expressive rhetoric or metaphoric language, an architecture without superfluous details in which the orientation becomes crucial through its form, structures and materials.

The generous use of natural light, a perfect organisation of the spaces, the choice of specific materials, and the careful orientation of the structures are the basic ingredients of this work full of order and balance. These three dwellings not only produce multiplicity, variety, potentiality and virtuality, but also a way of inhabiting and combining private and common spaces.

The elementary rhythm of the square-cube is added to the horizontal nature of the base on which the three dwellings are placed, creating an expressive and symphonic effect in which the different dimensions seem to mediate between the vertical and the horizontal, and between the solid and the void.

Stan Bolt
O'Sullivan House
Salcombe, Devon, UK

Photographs: Simon Cooke

This dwelling is in a privileged setting: a strip of land framed between slope covered with thick vegetation and a small cliff that drops down to the estuary of Salcombe. Formerly the plot was no more than a strip of grasslands that belonged to the neighbouring villages. When it was put up for sale, it was subjected to a long and complex series of planning problems. Finally, the conditions of the planning permission were that the cracks in the cliff had to be repaired to stabilise and maintain the slope of the coast, and all the materials and plants had to be transported by ship. The simple and functional design solution was conditioned by the need to respond pragmatically to these setbacks and by the desire to take advantage of the rich opportunities provided by the coastline. The desire to seek parameters such as panoramic views, light and reflections on the water led to a series of orchestrated interventions. Since the cliff required major repairs, it was stabilised by a concrete retaining wall that extended the cliff vertically up to the height of the vaulted roof of the dwelling.

Inside this protected environment, the building was conceived as a series of introverted "boxes" that provided refuge and privacy, combined with extroverted spaces that are structured according to the demands of the inhabitant and designed to favour spatial interconnection. This distinction between public and private spaces is articulated through the additional construction details and the use of different materials. The abundance of glazed areas, terraces, overhanging balconies and porches that continue the perspectives are a few of the elements that helped to erode the distinction between exterior and interior. On the other hand, the sense of "refuge" was nurtured through the different private rooms. These only open up toward the exterior through openings that provide selected views, as if they were pictures on the wall.

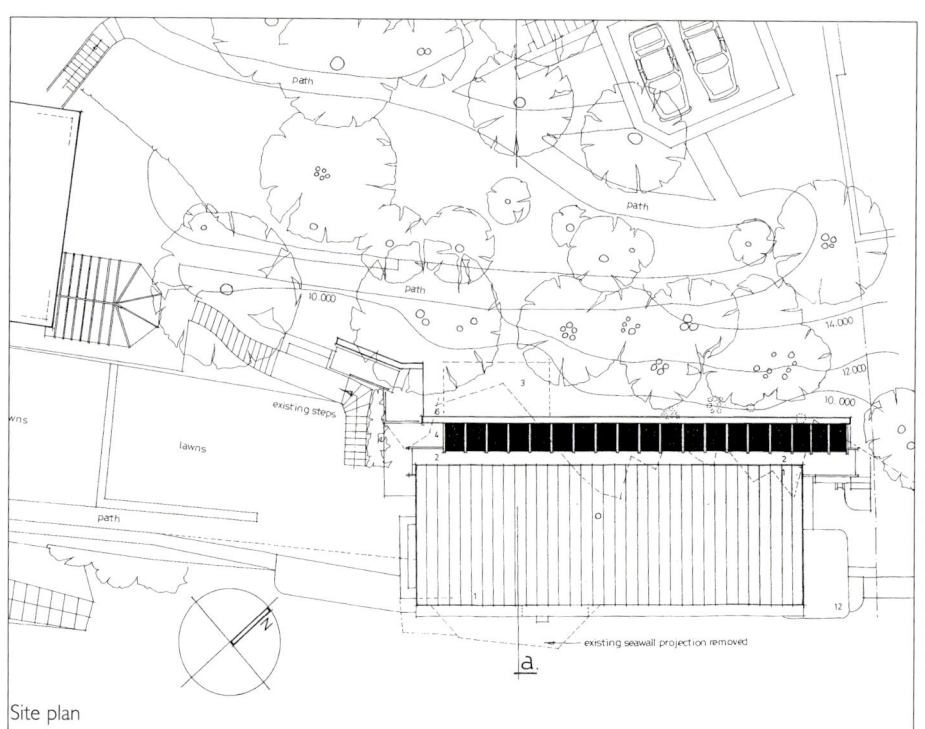

Site plan

The combination of different construction materials such as stone and wood gives the scheme an aesthetics that is not out of tune with the environment of the estuary in which is sited.

The roof and the volume set that is suspended over the water are the two architectural elements that most attract the attention at first sight.

The communication between the exterior and interior spaces was a basic element in the conception of this scheme. In order to take full advantage of its privileged situation, it was decided to create a garden and to add terraces and balconies at the different ends and levels of the building.

TEN Arquitectos
House IA
Valle Bravo, Mexico

Photographs: Luis Gordoa, Frank Visser

The architects Bernardo Gómez-Pimienta and Enrique Norten designed this dwelling, built on a hillside in the Bravo Valley overlooking a lake, with the aim of creating a space in which the beauty of the landscape was a positive feature but presented no obstacle to the distinctive character of the scheme. The site has stone walls covered with earth and gravel, and it was decided to maintain these fragments unfinished and to place a glass prism on them. The heights of these walls thus define the levels of the project. The building has a series of strips parallel to the lake and perpendicular to the slope that define the different platforms of the interior and the exterior spaces.

The glass volume of Cartesian clarity and strict order organises the architectural programme by means of its structure, because it houses the living room, the dining room and the main bedroom, all separated by a low volume that contains the service areas. This glass prism sits on a stone base in which two bedrooms are located. The living room window runs along the facade, opening the space toward the exterior and the lake.

The wooden ceiling is supported by thin columns, which makes it seem to float on the interior walls without touching them, thus creating spatial continuity. The sloping roof responds to the demands of the urban regulations. Its northern aspect was used to extend it toward the exterior by means of a wooden pergola, thus creating a sun filter with views of the lake. The floor is also extended toward the courtyard, and its intersection with the pergola forms the inhabited space. This solution also makes it possible to expand the internal space outwards and thus to eliminate the limit between interior and exterior.

A minimum number of materials was used for the construction of this dwelling and the colours were chosen to enhance the exterior (the lake, the mountains and the sky), and to emphasise the changes in the vegetation and the landscape.

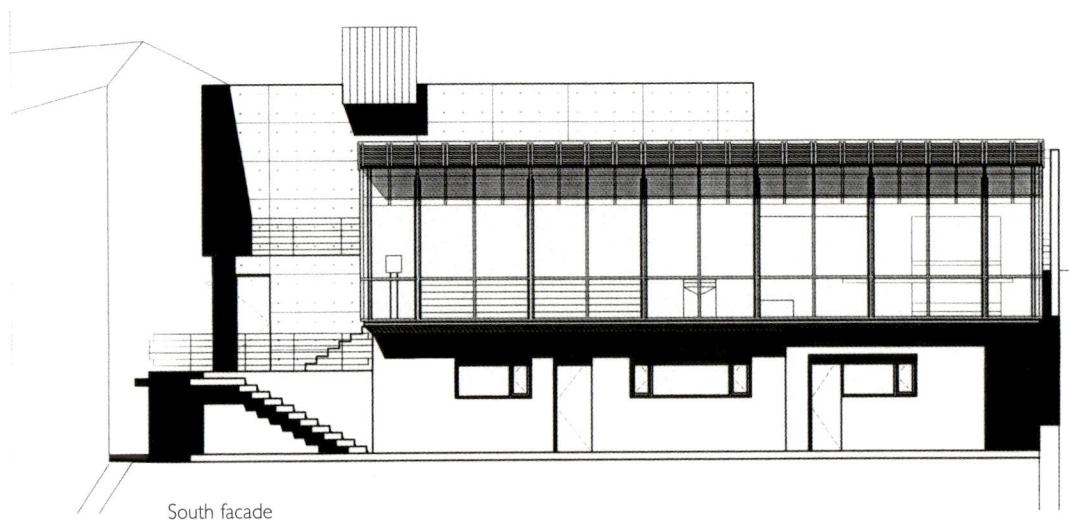

South facade

The glass volume, which is both transparent and translucent, offers a continuous view and creates a play of transparencies and opacities that varies according to the time of day, as it absorbs and reflects the colours of the exterior.

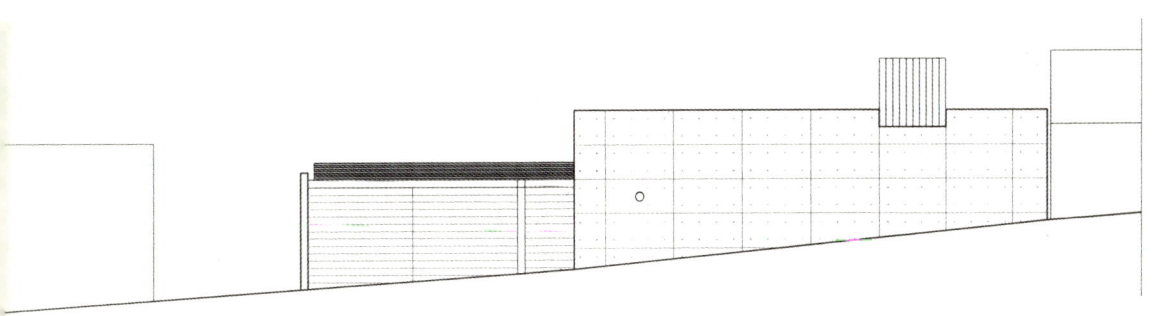

North facade

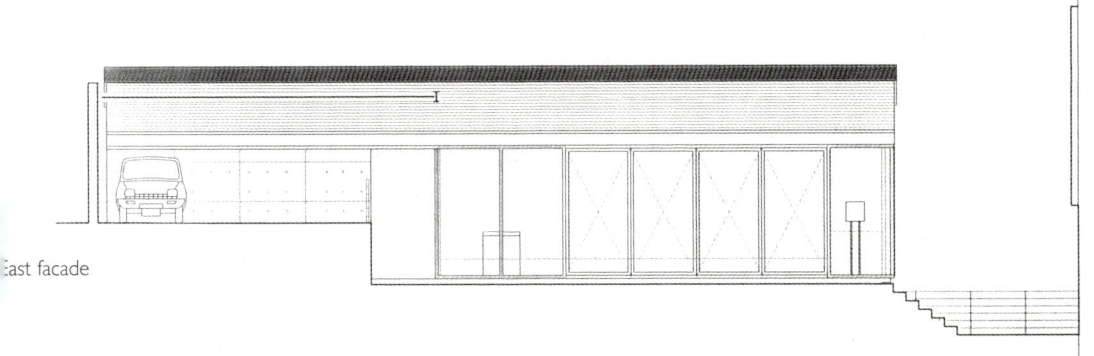

East facade

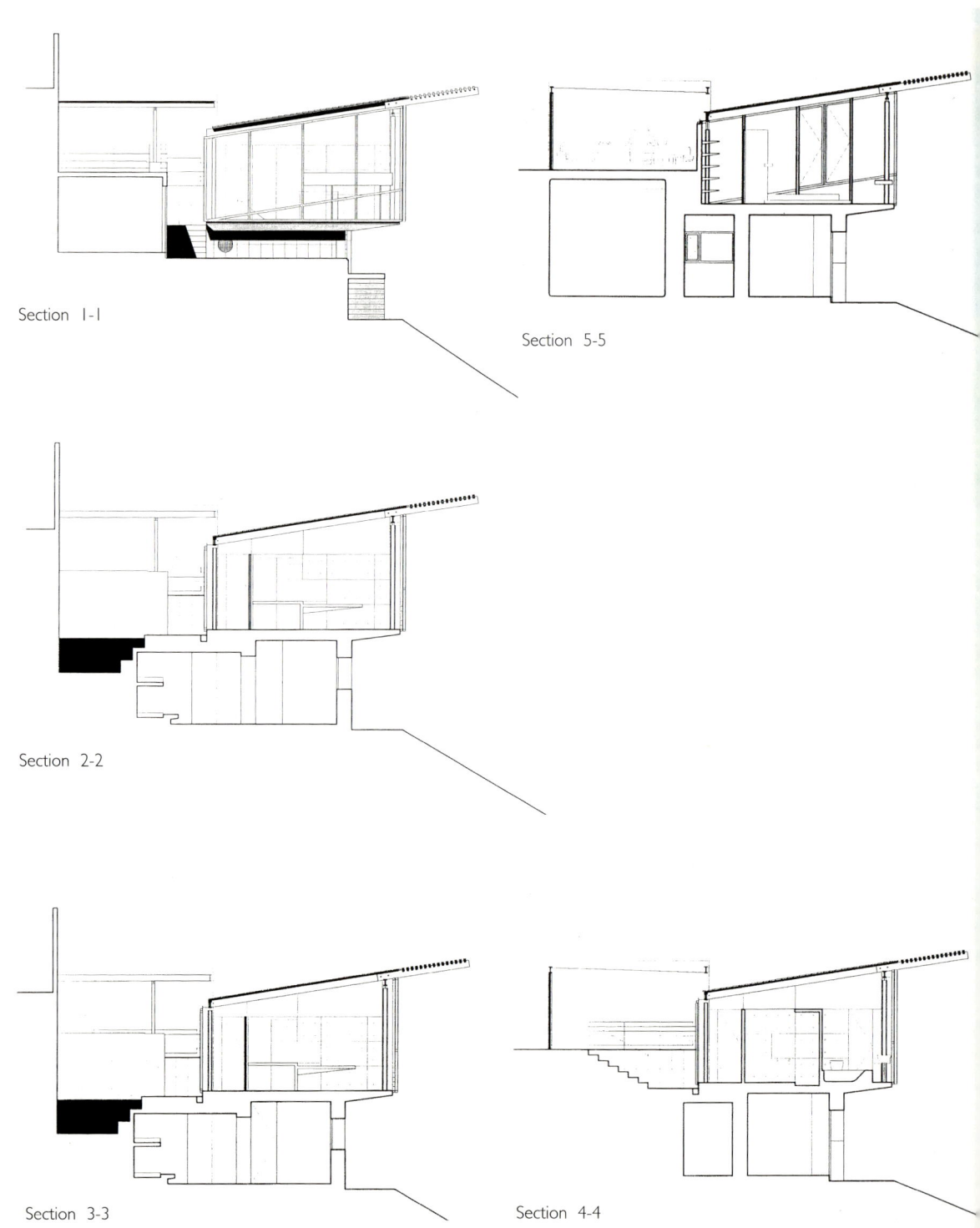
Section 1-1

Section 5-5

Section 2-2

Section 3-3

Section 4-4

Toshiko Mori
Cohen House
Casey Key, Florida, USA

Photographs: Paul Warchol

This building —a guest house for a dwelling designed by Paul Rudolph in 1957— is located on an extensive sand bank framed by the Gulf of Mexico to the west and the Sarasota Bay to the east. This auxiliary house was built on the traces of an old structure destroyed by a hurricane. Though the area is exposed to an extreme climate —hurricanes, tides, cloudbursts, and strong sunlight— it is an authentic paradise inhabited by turtles and other marine animals. To protect it from the high tide and the violent storms, the dwelling was raised 5 metres above sea level. It is surrounded by the oaks, palms and tropical trees that grow on the site, and is accessed by an external staircase of stainless steel. This staircase becomes the new "centre" of the house, connecting and separating the activities in the interior.

The construction responds to the intensity of the climate with concrete foundations and pillars buried 6ft deep in the sand. The dwelling is thus able to use the presence of vegetation to increase its possibilities: the volume of the building is immersed in the density of treetops that provide shade and privacy. To support the weight of the structure, in which concrete is the main material, walls and tubular steel columns were added to the pillars. Outwardly, the building shows wide glazed areas with different degrees of transparency, depending on the needs of the interior for protection against the blinding light and the intense heat. These different opacities create variety and give life to the facade, which would otherwise have seemed a simple hermetic glass box.

The design was conceived as a tribute to the legacy of the "Sarasota School", a group of architects led by Rudolph and Ralph Twichell that practised in the area from the early forties to the mid-sixties.

As it is high, the dwelling is protected from the tides and storms, establishes a better visual contact with the environment and takes advantage of the abundant presence of trees to gain shady spaces.

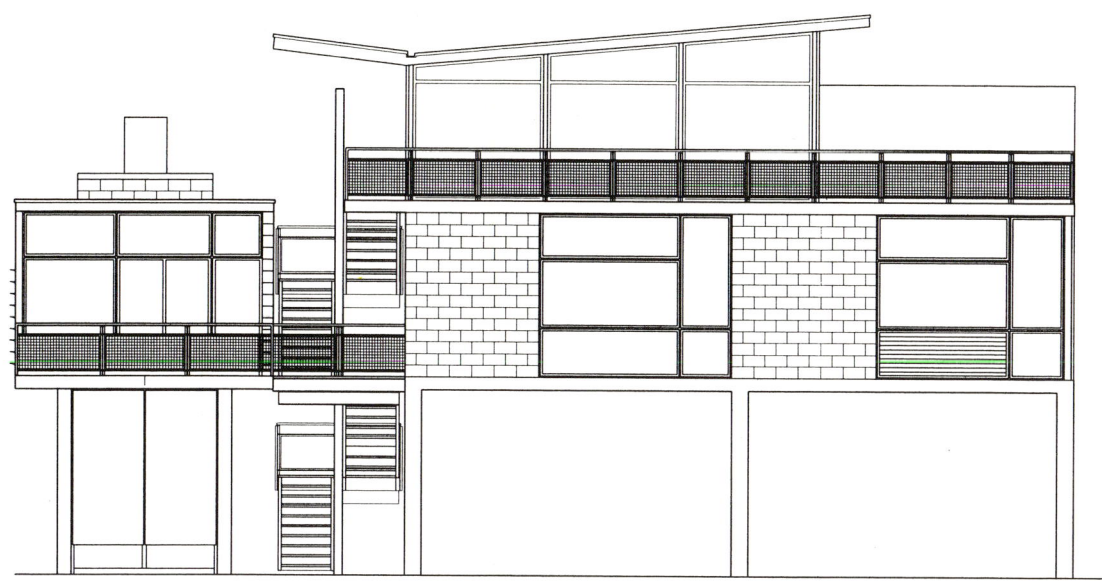

South elevation

255